Praise for *The Rudy in You*

"The authors' straightforward advice may seem obvious, but Phillips, Leddy and Ruettiger go further, providing solid examples of how to put these principles into practice. And for all the character building, they also appreciate that kids just want to have fun."

Kirkus Discoveries

"Excellent! *The Rudy in You* is filled with timeless principles dearly needed in today's society. Every kid, parent, and coach involved in American youth sports should own this book."

Grant Teaff
Executive Director,
American Football Coaches Association

"Everyone involved in youth sports should read this book and put into practice the lessons in it. I highly recommend it!"

Jon Butler
Executive Director,
Pop Warner Football

"If every parent and youth sports coach practiced the fundamentals set out in this book, all children would enjoy quality youth sports experiences that nurture their dreams and help them become citizens of tomorrow."

Joel Mark
National President,
American Youth Soccer Organization (AYSO)

"This book is a brilliant and innovative concept that will go far in helping children benefit from a positive experience in youth sports. I believe it is destined to become a classic."

Bo Mitchell
President and Cofounder (with Garth Brooks),
Teammates for Kids Foundation

The Rudy in You will help young athletes, their parents, and coaches learn how to become more Rudy-like. Since we all need a little more Rudy in us, these pages are an outstanding guide for everyone involved in youth sports and everyone interested in elevating the role of sportsmanship in our communities."

Greg Aiello
Vice President of Public Relations,
National Football League

"Terrific! These lessons from the story of Rudy Ruettiger's life are timeless principles that will inspire and guide both young people and adults. Like the movie *Rudy*, *The Rudy in You* will be around for a long time to come. It will stand the test of time."

Angelo Pizzo
Producer and Screenwriter,
Hoosiers, Rudy, The Game of Their Lives

"The coaches' section of this book is one of the best pieces on coaching I've ever read. Including parents and players with the coaches is a new and different approach. I'm surprised no one else has ever thought of it."

John Gruden
Head Coach,
Tampa Bay Buccaneers

"The Rudy in You contains many of the lessons and values taught to me by my parents and coaches when I was growing up. They made a difference in my life, and I believe they'll make a difference in the lives of countless kids all across America. This book is destined to be around for a long time. It's timeless."

> Greg Maddux
> Pitcher,
> Chicago Cubs
> Four-time winner of the Cy Young Award

"As adults, we need inspiration. *The Rudy in You* will help us focus on what our goals as parents and/or coaches should be. In my clinical setting, I see people struggling with problems that would not be as pronounced if the principles and values in this book had been more a part of their lives."

> Dr. W. Scott West
> General Practice Physician
> Nashville, Tennessee

"The Rudy in You is right on when it comes to kids. In the state of Michigan, we work with over a million students each year. We try to provide them with material they can relate to. This book could be a critical part of our resource material."

> Paul C. Bergan
> President,
> Michigan Council of Vocational Administrators
> Member of Michigan High School Football
> Coaches Association Hall of Fame

The Rudy in You

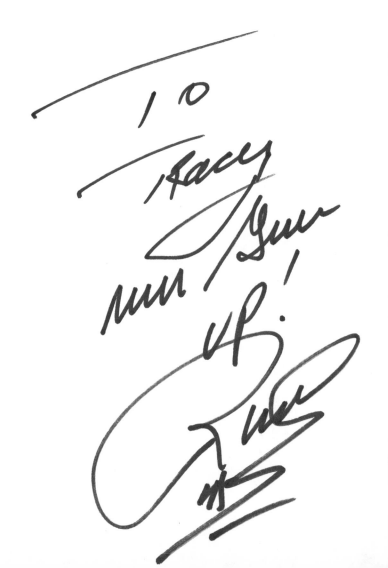

The Rudy in You

◆

A Guide to Building Teamwork, Fair Play and Good Sportsmanship for Young Athletes, Parents and Coaches

by
Donald T. Phillips,
Rudy Ruettiger,
Peter M. Leddy, PhD

iUniverse Star
New York Lincoln Shanghai

The Rudy in You
A Guide to Building Teamwork, Fair Play and Good Sportsmanship for Young Athletes, Parents and Coaches

iUniverse Star
an iUniverse, Inc. imprint

iUniverse books may be ordered through booksellers or by contacting:

iUniverse
2021 Pine Lake Road, Suite 100
Lincoln, NE 68512
www.iuniverse.com
1-800-Authors (1-800-288-4677)

ISBN-13: 978-1-58348-764-8 (pbk)
ISBN-13: 978-0-595-81113-7 (ebk)
ISBN-10: 1-58348-764-6 (pbk)
ISBN-10: 0-595-81113-2 (ebk)

Printed in the United States of America

Contents

Preface

On the evening news not long ago, we began to see some troubling trends in behavior at youth sporting events—parents getting into fights with referees, coaches screaming at kids, and worse. In personal experiences with our own children, we saw similar disturbing and disrespectful behavior. It became clear that many parents and coaches had not aligned themselves with what youth sports should be all about. So we decided to do something about it. Our collaboration on this book is the result.

All three of us have been involved in youth sports for most of our lives. We participated when we were children, we became parents and signed up our own kids, and we coached our kids' teams. Each of us also brings professional expertise (beyond our experience with youth sports) to the table to make this book something special. Don Phillips is a writer who has studied leadership extensively, including that of several great sports coaches. Rudy, the subject of the hit motion picture *Rudy*, was the little kid who had a dream and achieved it. During his youth, he experienced both good and bad coaches, but with the help of his well-grounded parents, he was able to become a model for success. And Pete Leddy's training in human behavior provides skilled analysis into the wants, needs, and desires of young people, parents, and coaches. He has also conducted detailed studies about what coaches do right and what they do wrong.

From the very beginning, we concentrated on the three main groups of people that youth sports comprise: the kids themselves, their parents, and their coaches. Most books and pamphlets on this subject deal independently with either the parents or the coaches. Very few books speak directly to the kids. And none that we know of deal with all three groups together.

Yet the fate of children in sports lies directly in the hands of their parents, their coaches, and to a lesser degree, themselves. So we divided the book into three sections, each tailored and written to a specific audience. The coaches' section tends to be a little more technical, for instance, and the players' section a bit more simply worded. The kids' section is presented first, because we believe the kids come first in youth athletics. The parents' section is located in the middle because parents are central to the success of their children's involvement in youth sports, and because they are a buffer between their children and the coaches. The coaches' section is presented last because they're the anchor—and because they can make or break a kid's experience in youth sports.

In this book, kids learn about responsibility, self-awareness, and the fundamental link between their own personal behavior and the success of the team. And they learn about the fun of having a dream—just like Rudy Ruettiger did.

Parents are advised to focus on guiding their kids and providing unconditional love and support. In our second section, parents will read some core psychological insights, such as the fact that kids have an unbelievable need to feel part of a group. It's as essential as getting protein or carbohydrates. In order to grow, young people simply need to feel a certain level of significance in whatever they're doing.

In their section, coaches receive tips on how to walk the fine line of managing for inclusion without being all-inclusive. They learn how to make each child feel he or she has a significant role in the team's success, regardless of whether the child plays the entire game or only one minute of it.

Youth sports can play a significant role in the development of every child who participates. And it behooves parents, coaches, and the kids themselves to look at this time in their lives as one of physical, mental, and spiritual development. Time spent in youth sports can help children grow into responsible adults who know the difference between competitiveness and violence, between teamwork and selfishness, between right and wrong.

We hope this small book will provide useful guidance for the adults who coach kids, for the parents who are trying to do a good job raising their kids, and for the kids themselves, so that they can really have a fun and enjoyable experience.

Rudy Ruettiger wasn't the most talented kid on his team. But with hard work, desire, and a positive experience in youth sports, the little guy overcame all kinds of obstacles to realize his big dream. Through it all, he remained a good and decent person who reached deep within himself to pull out the best he had to offer.

There is a Rudy in everybody. And it's up to all of us to bring it out in each and every child. That's what *The Rudy in You* is all about. It's about the kids.

Don Phillips
Rudy Ruettiger
Pete Leddy

A generous portion of author royalties are donated to the Rudy Ruettiger Foundation.

Part I

Players

You can do anything. You can go anywhere.
You can be anybody or anything you want to be.

Chapter 1
Dreaming Big

Rudy Ruettiger wasn't a very big guy. He was only 5 feet 7 inches tall. He didn't weigh very much either—only 165 pounds. Even though he was small, Rudy had a big dream. He wanted to play football at one of the most prestigious colleges in the United States—the University of Notre Dame.

At that time, Notre Dame had one of the best football programs in the nation—with a tradition that stretched back more than half a century to the legendary days of Coach Knute Rockne. The football team was always in contention for the national championship. But the average size of a Notre Dame football player was about 6 feet 2 inches, 220 pounds. That meant Rudy was more than half a foot shorter and weighed 55 pounds less than an average player.

Some people told Rudy that he was crazy—that he would never make it. They told him to get another dream—one that was possible. But Rudy refused to give up. He was accepted to Notre Dame even though he had poor grades in high school. He made the football team even though he was the smallest guy out there. And although he played in only one game, for only twenty-seven seconds, and got only one tackle—Rudy Ruettiger is today the most famous football player in the history of the University of Notre Dame. They even made a movie about him.

How did all that happen?

Well, there was something inside Rudy that helped him become a winner. That something is inside all of us. And you don't have to look very far to find the Rudy in you. All you have to do is read on.

Figure Out Your "Want To"

The first thing you should do is figure out your "want to."

What is a "want to," you ask? That's your dream. That's what you "want to" be. It's what you "want to" do. When Rudy was a kid, he told his dad, "I 'want to' play football for the University of Notre Dame." From then on, he had something to shoot for, something to work for, something to have fun with. Having a dream is a good thing. It's also a healthy thing, especially for kids. And the bigger the dream, the better.

So what do *you* want to do? What is *your* dream? Remember, you can do anything, you can go anywhere, you can be anybody or anything you want to be. Think about it for a while. Use your imagination.

If you already know what your "want to" is, it would be a good idea to mention it to your parents. Say to them: "Mom, Dad, I really want to play soccer [or volleyball, or hockey, or whatever sport it is]." See what they have to say about it. They'll probably encourage you to get started.

If you don't know what your "want to" is, try some different things. Take a crack at something that interests you. Ask your parents what they think. After all, they've known you for your whole life, haven't they? They probably know what you like and what you don't like. They may have some good ideas. "I think you'd really like basketball," they might say, "or tennis, perhaps."

Actually, it might not be a sport at all that interests you. It might be singing or acting or computers or chess. And you should pursue those things if they really interest you. But because this is a book about youth athletics, we'll use various sports as our examples.

The important thing to remember, though, is that you should get involved in something. As you look at different things, remember to be sensitive to your feelings and your instincts. Whatever you try, make sure it's something that sounds fun and interesting to you.

The first thing you try might not end up being your "want to." For instance, football was not the first thing that interested Rudy. He actually started with baseball. Rudy got excited about the uniform, the glove, and playing with a bunch of kids his own age. And he really liked playing baseball. It was great fun.

But then Rudy tried football and he felt something different, something great. He soon realized that this was something he would love for the rest of his life. Football became his passion, his lifelong dream. Playing football at Notre Dame became Rudy's "want to."

Work on Your "Have To"

After you figure out your "want to," it's time to answer the question, "What do I 'have to' do to make it happen?"

It will help to do some research. Read a book on the subject. Ask some successful people how they achieved their dreams. Or start by asking your parents for their advice. They might surprise you with their knowledge. They might say: "Okay, if you want to play second base, you need to practice ground balls. You need to learn the position inside out. You need to practice all the situations that involve the second baseman."

Once Rudy finished his research, he actually made a written list of his "have to's":

1. Get accepted to Notre Dame.

2. Make the football team.

3. Get in the game and play.

That's a simple list, right? Of course it is. But what do you do if one of your "have to's" seems so big that it's out of reach? Well, you don't give up before you've even started. The first thing to do is to make another list—this time of smaller "have to's" that will help you get to your bigger "have to." The smaller ones will be easier. You can knock them off one by one and then, before you know it, you will have achieved your big "have to."

That's the way Rudy did it. For instance, in order to get accepted to Notre Dame, Rudy had to go to a junior college and make good grades. Then, because he had a learning disability, he had to work harder than everybody else to get those good grades.

Also, once he got accepted to Notre Dame, Rudy would have to try out for the football team. In order to make the team, he'd have to go to tryouts and convince the coaches that he could play with the bigger athletes.

After he made the team, in order to play, Rudy knew he'd have to work harder than all the rest once again. He'd have to go to every practice, show the team his heart and his character, and do everything that was asked of him.

Sometimes it was hard for Rudy. But he stuck with it because he realized that if he "wanted to" be a part of that great Notre Dame tradition, he would "have to" do all the things on his list.

So make a list of "have to's" to get to your "want to." Be sure the things on the list are realistic—things you really can achieve. And also make sure that they are measurable—so you can see progress along the way.

Make a Commitment

Once you start on the path to achieving your dream, you need to promise yourself that you will not give up just because your "have to's" seem too hard. That's called making a commitment.

Think about Rudy again.

When he got into junior college at Holy Cross, he had a really, really tough time making good grades. At times, he wanted to give up because it was just too difficult. But Rudy knew if he didn't finish the year, he would have absolutely no chance of getting accepted to Notre Dame. In addition, Rudy had made a commitment and he was determined to stick with it. So he finished the year at Holy Cross even though it was very hard to do.

One of the things on your list of "have to's" might be that you play one season of soccer with a certain team. So you sign up with the team and you start the season. But suppose the practices are tougher than you thought they would be. Suppose you don't particularly like the coach or some of the other players. Suppose you find that you didn't make the starting team.

Many kids would think of giving up—of quitting before the season is over. But not you. You're not going to quit before the season is over because you have made a commitment. It may be tough on you, but you're staying. And by sticking with it, you may find that, over the rest of the season, things can change. You may find that your coach isn't so bad after all. You may actually make the starting team halfway through the season. And you may get used to those tough practices and also come to realize that they have made you a better player.

At the end of the year, you may decide that it's time to try a different team. And that's okay, because you stayed the entire season. You kept your commitment and now it's time to make a decision on what you want to do next.

Many kids who try new things quit too easily. And when they become adults, they end up never finishing anything.

By learning to commit, you automatically develop perseverance. And what is perseverance?

Perseverance is the quality of never giving up, of standing strong when things aren't going your way, of having courage. Perseverance is one of the qualities that all successful people possess. They do not quit when the going gets tough.

Things to Remember
1/Dreaming Big

- Get a dream. Figure out your "want to."
- If you already know what your "want to" is, mention it to your parents.
- If you don't know, try some different things that sound fun and interesting.
- Be sure to get involved in something.
- Do some research. Read a book. Ask some successful people how they achieved their dreams.
- Make a written list of your "have to's."
- Be sure the things on your list are realistic and measurable.
- Once you start, promise yourself that you will not give up just because your "have to's" seem too hard.
- Keep your commitment through the entire season.
- When you commit, you automatically develop perseverance.
- Perseverance is the quality of never giving up, of standing strong when things aren't going your way, of having courage.
- Successful people never quit when the going gets tough.

Begin your journey quietly.
Take the high road—the road
of character that leads to success.

Chapter 2
Listening and Learning

Rudy Ruettiger was a dreamer. He wanted to be recognized. He wanted to be somebody. And that's okay. It's not only normal, it also gives a person something to strive for.

But most people who are dreamers are not doers. They don't achieve their dreams because they don't do anything about them. Rudy, however, was both a dreamer and a doer. He had a dream and he did something about it. That's why he was a champion.

Rudy's journey to success began quietly. He didn't talk very much. He listened, he learned, and he was patient. The path he took was a special road. It was the high road. The high road of honesty and integrity. The road of character that leads to success.

Respect Your Coach and the Sport

Having respect for people is an important part of achieving your dream. What does it mean when you have respect for others? It means you believe that they have value and are important. It means you care about them. You are considerate of their feelings and what they have to say. It means you act courteously toward them. When you respect people, you always treat them with the Golden Rule: "Treat others as you would have them treat you."

Don't forget that respecting other people reflects positively on you. It shows everybody that you are a good person. Your coach, especially, needs to know you are a good person because he or she is the one who is going to guide and teach you. If your coach doesn't have confidence in you, it can hurt your performance. So pay attention to your coach. Listen to what he or she is saying. Never, ever talk when your coach is talking. And always look your coach in the eye.

Remember that you cannot just show up and say, "Okay, coach me!" It doesn't work that way. You have to be coachable. To be coachable, you have to earn your coach's respect. And to earn your coach's respect, you must first show respect for your coach.

Keep in mind, also, that respect doesn't stop with people. You should also have respect for the sport you are playing. You should hold it in high regard, honor it, and understand that many people have played this sport for many years because it is a worthy endeavor.

So learn the rules of your sport. Learn the fundamentals. If you think about it, that should be one of your "have to's" anyway. How can you possibly achieve your "want to" if you don't clearly understand everything there is to know about your sport?

Once you find a position that you really enjoy, study that position. For example, a soccer goalie's purpose is to keep the ball from going into the net. That sounds simple, but it's also basic. Any person who wants to be a good goalie must know that.

Next, you should learn everything there is to know about playing your position. When should a goalie go out toward the ball or stay back near the net? Where should a goalie stand during a corner kick or on a penalty kick? And so on. Listen to people who are good at that position. Watch them during a game, and then practice what you have learned. Remember, if you don't *apply* these lessons so that you improve, you will not be able to achieve your "want to."

Work Hard

Very few people become successful without having worked hard for it. That is especially true in sports, where the athletes who make it look easy are usually the ones who work the hardest.

The best players go to practice. As a matter of fact, they never miss a practice. And nobody, but *nobody* has a better work ethic. So if you want to be a good player, if you want to achieve your dream, then get out there and invest the time. Go through the steps. Get better at your position. Practice! Practice! Practice!

Everybody knows, however, that practice is not always fun. Sometimes you have to do things that you don't necessarily like to do. Sometimes it can be dreary. Sometimes you feel too tired. But if you want to succeed, you must get up and do it anyway. That's called discipline.

The great basketball coach Mike Krzyzewski (Coach K) from Duke University says that discipline is nothing more than "doing what you are supposed to do in the best possible manner at the time you are supposed to do it." That doesn't sound so bad, now does it?

Actually, discipline can be very good when done the right way. It's just like when you're in school. When the teachers have a lot of kids together, their activities have structure. They are organized. Discipline, in many ways, is about having organized fun. So don't goof off during practice. Listen and be a part of the team.

Hard work is a very important part of a person's character. So work hard and show your coach, your parents, and your teammates what you're made of. Impress them and earn their respect so that they'll all point to you and say, "There's the kid who works the hardest."

Be Patient and Flexible

How many players are perfect at their positions when they set foot on the field of play for the first time? How many people are great at something they have just started? Doesn't it take practice and hard work to be able to do anything really well?

Just look at how many times Rudy failed. He was rejected by Notre Dame on his first try. Once he got in and made the football team, he constantly got knocked down in practice by the bigger guys. Then he had to spend two full seasons on the practice squad. He couldn't dress for games. He couldn't run through the tunnel onto the field with the other players. Heck, the little guy couldn't even ride the bench.

For Rudy, failure and rejection were almost a given. The first couple of times he failed, it was tough for him—even heartbreaking. But then Rudy got tough. He realized that some people take a little more time to develop than others. Some players become starters right away. Others don't. But that doesn't mean they quit the team. Just like Rudy, they learn to have patience.

And what is patience? Patience is the ability to calmly wait without complaining. It's a kind of steady endurance when you're trying to get something done. And it's being kind to other people who may not move as fast as you do. All players with a dream should learn to have patience. Patience with their teammates, patience with their coach, and most important of all, patience with themselves.

Flexibility is another important principle for players. They need to be ready to change, if necessary. Not the dream itself, but the plan to get there can and should change often. For instance, sometimes one of the items in your plan may not work after you try it. But there is often more than one path you can take to achieve your dream. In fact, there may be several paths you can take at the same time.

Rudy was a pretty flexible guy when you think about it. On his list of "have to's" was the goal of doing something directly for the football team during the season, even though he wasn't yet registered at Notre Dame. So he showed up near the end of a practice just as all the players were jogging off the practice field. He ran after them and shouted to the coach, "If there's anything I can do to help the team, you just let me know."

But that didn't get him anywhere. In fact, he was run over by the team and fell to the ground. But Rudy got up and decided maybe that was one "have to" that wouldn't necessarily help him get to his dream. Instead he decided to join one of Notre Dame's student activities—the Football Boosters. This was the group that organized the pep rallies and painted the football helmets gold before each game. But when they found out he was not a student at the university, he wasn't allowed to be in the organization.

So Rudy next decided to try to become the assistant to the janitor in charge of the football field and locker rooms. And with this move, Rudy's luck changed—because the janitor, whose name was Fortune, decided to give Rudy the job. And if you've watched the movie, you know how much being around Fortune helped Rudy achieve his dream.

The lesson here is that Rudy was flexible with his "have to's." He was also patient, wasn't he? Well, patience and flexibility are part of a player's preparation for success. If you are a winner like Rudy, you never stop training, working, or practicing. You always believe that some how, some way, some day, your opportunity will come. And when that opportunity comes, you will be ready for it.

Things to Remember

2/Listening and Learning

- Be both a dreamer and a doer.
- Respect people by always treating them with the Golden Rule: "Treat others as you would have them treat you."
- Respect your coach. Pay attention. Don't talk when your coach is talking. Always look your coach in the eye.
- Remember that respect doesn't stop with people. You should also have respect for the sport you are playing.
- Learn the rules and fundamentals of your sport—and learn everything there is to know about playing your position.
- Remember, athletes who make it look easy are usually the ones who work the hardest.
- The best players never miss a practice—and they don't goof off during practice.
- Hard work is a very important part of a person's character.
- Patience is the ability to calmly wait without complaining. It's a kind of steady endurance when you're trying to get something done.
- Have patience with your teammates, with your coach, and, most importantly, with yourself.
- There is often more than one path you can take to achieve your dream. So be ready to change if necessary. Be flexible with your "want to's."
- Always believe that some how, some way, some day—your opportunity will come. And you will be ready for it.

Let go of what happened five minutes ago.
The next play is the most important play.

Chapter 3
Having a Positive Attitude

When Rudy began to talk about his dream, many people were extremely negative. "Be realistic, Rudy," they said. "Your family's not rich. You're not a great athlete. Only smart kids go to Notre Dame. Your grades are too low. Your SAT scores are too low. You don't have a chance. Get real, Rudy."

Some of those people wanted to see Rudy fail because of petty jealousy or a "who do you think you are" kind of attitude. For others, being negative toward Rudy was an excuse for not succeeding themselves. They didn't want to try because they were afraid to take the risk. If Rudy succeeded, it would make them feel bad. Still other people simply had a negative attitude toward everything in life.

Successful people, however, learn how to turn off the negative. Rudy trained himself to listen to the positive side. People used to say to him, "Rudy, you don't hear the word 'no!'"

"You're right," he would respond. "I don't hear your negative attitude."

When Rudy said that, he was acting like an All-American athlete when he really wasn't one. He was exhibiting a positive attitude. And a positive attitude is critical if you want to achieve your dream.

Surround Yourself with Positive People

It's not easy to have a positive outlook all the time. And there were days when Rudy was down, when he felt he would never be successful. "I'm a failure," he once told his best friend.

"No, you're not, Rudy," came the reply. "You're not a failure. Those other people who are saying you can't do it—they're just a bunch of squirrels. They don't know the real you."

A couple of days later, on Rudy's birthday, Rudy's best friend gave him a Notre Dame jacket. "You were born to wear that jacket," he said.

That made Rudy feel great. Just knowing that somebody believed in him that much gave him a lot of hope. And that's when Rudy realized it would be smart to have people around him who were encouraging, rather than discouraging. So he decided not to hang around whiners and complainers. He avoided the pity parties that so many players used to bad-mouth their coach or to complain about not being on the starting team.

Rudy also decided to focus on the positive things people said to him. He knew that everybody says both helpful and unhelpful things. From then on, Rudy picked out the good stuff people said to him—and he ignored the bad stuff.

While Rudy was pursuing his dream, many positive and constructive people came into his life. They were of different ages and came from all walks of life. They knew something about the sport he was in, the position he wanted to play, and the goal he had set for himself. They not only told him the agreeable stuff that made him feel good, they also told him the truth about things that were hard to hear. They explained *why* he wasn't succeeding. "It's because you haven't done *this* or because you haven't done *that*," they said. "It's because you're in a period where you've been more lazy than energetic."

These were people who told Rudy the truth even when it hurt. These were Rudy's *real* friends. If you are going to be successful, you need to cultivate friendships with positive, constructive people. And once you've found them, you need to *listen* to them—just like Rudy did.

One of Rudy's best friends turned out to be the janitor, Fortune. He was kind, he was decent, and he was crusty. But he never let Rudy sink into a valley of depression. If Rudy started to whine or complain, Fortune gave him a reality check.

For instance, when Rudy mentioned that he wanted to become an All-American college football player, Fortune advised him to be honest with himself and to be a little more reasonable. "You're simply too small to be an All-American, Rudy," he said. "It's just not realistic. But that doesn't mean you can't achieve your dream. No, sir! You can still be on the team. You can still graduate from this university with a degree."

Fortune also pointed out Rudy's strengths as well as his weaknesses. "You have a lot of heart, Rudy—more than most players," he said. "And that will take you a long way. The simple fact that you never give up and never give in will greatly increase your chances of success." Rudy always knew that he had to work hard to overcome his weaknesses. But Fortune reminded him that he should also play upon his strengths and let them work for him.

Shake It Off

Suppose you're playing second base and you let a grounder go through your legs which, in turn, allows a couple of runs to score. It's a normal reaction to feel bad about that—to be dejected or mad at yourself. But you can't let it affect you for too long, can you? There's another batter stepping up to the plate right away. If that batter sees that you are upset, then the next ball might be coming straight toward you on purpose. So you have to put the mistake behind you as fast as you possibly can.

Now think about this: In baseball and softball, when a player makes a mistake, it's not called "the end of the world," is it? And it's not called "the end of your dream," either. It is simply called an "error." Remember, an error is just a mistake.

In life, everybody makes mistakes. And in sports, everybody makes errors. But the best athletes do not think too long about their errors. They can't afford to. If they let every error get the best of them, then they never have a good game—and the next thing they know, they're on the bench.

If you're going to be successful, you have to do the same thing. In a game, you have to put the error behind you right away. You must think, "The next play is the most important play." And in life, if you make a mistake on the way to your dream, you simply put it behind you. You have to let go of what happened five minutes ago and start thinking about the next play.

After a player has made an error, did you ever hear somebody call out, "Shake it off! Shake it off!"? Well, that's an old saying in almost all sports. And do you know where that saying originated? It came from the Bible.

When Jesus sent out the twelve apostles to spread the word of the Gospel, he encouraged them to knock on every door in the city. If they were received kindly, that was great. But if they were rejected, Jesus advised them to "shake the dust off their feet" and move on.

That's good advice for everybody. "Shake it off and move on."

Have a positive attitude and move on. And remember that the only person stopping you is yourself.

Have Pride

If you are someone who listens a lot (and you should be), you often hear people talking about pride. "I have a lot of pride in what I do." "I'm proud of this team." "Make me proud of you."

Did you ever stop a minute to think about what being proud really means? Well, pride is a feeling you get when you're part of something good. Sometimes it starts with your uniform. You tuck in your jersey. You wear your hat straight. The letter on your hat and the words on your jersey mean something to you. Your uniform symbolizes something strong, something good. It lets you know that you are part of something bigger than yourself, something bigger than any one person, something important.

Pride is also the feeling you get when you think about all the hard work you've put in. There's pride in the running, in the hustling, in the discipline. You've done something most people haven't done. You're satisfied with your effort. It really means a lot to you.

People who have pride feel that they are involved in a *worthy* endeavor. It's worth their time. It provides them with self-respect, dignity, and satisfaction. And when you have all that, it makes you feel good. You don't want to lose it.

Pride had a lot to do with Rudy Ruettiger's success.

When Rudy was on the practice squad for the football team, he got to wear a uniform. And that uniform—that jersey, that gold helmet, those pads—*really* meant something to him.

For the longest time, he only was able to wear the uniform at practices. But that was enough to keep him going. During all the times he wasn't recognized for his efforts, or the times he didn't get to play, Rudy's pride in being part of the University of Notre Dame kept him going. It motivated him to try again and again and again.

He wanted to dress in the locker room with the other starters, to run through that tunnel onto the field, to play in just one game in front of a home-team crowd, to hear the Notre Dame fight song after his team scored. Now *that* would be a proud moment!

Pride is a very positive thing. It tells you how far you've come—and how far you can go. It lets you know that no matter how negative a situation may be, there is always something positive that can come out of it. Pride helps you keep things in perspective. It gives you self-respect and reminds you that life is good.

You're a player. You're part of a team. Take pride in it.

Things to Remember

3/Having a Positive Attitude

- Successful people learn to turn off the negative attitudes.
- Just knowing that somebody believes in you can give you a lot of hope.
- It's smart to have people around you who are encouraging rather than discouraging. Surround yourself with positive people.
- Don't hang around whiners and complainers. Avoid pity parties.
- Listen to friends who will tell you the truth even when it hurts.
- Get a reality check once in a while. Remind yourself to be realistic about your "want to's."
- It's important to overcome your weaknesses. But you should also use your strengths and let them work for you.
- If you let every error get the best of you, you will end up on the bench.
- Forget what happened five minutes ago and start thinking about the next play.
- If you get rejected, or you make a mistake, shake it off and move on.
- Pride is a feeling you get when you're part of something good, when you are involved in a worthy endeavor. It gives you self-respect, dignity, and satisfaction.
- Take pride in whatever you do. It will inspire you to do even more.

The best players give up the ball. They are more givers than takers. They also have the most friends.

Chapter 4
Building Relationships and Making Friends

To be successful in a team sport, you have to make good friends with your teammates and have good relationships with your coaches and parents. Why? Because on teams, people have to rely on each other to get things done. You can't do everything yourself. You're going to need help.

Friends help each other, don't they? Isn't that what friends are for?

Think about it for a moment. Don't you want to help your friends succeed? Well, it works both ways. Your friends want to help you too. They want you to succeed. So the more friends you have, the more people there will be who are on your side trying to help you achieve your dream. It's smart to make friends with everybody on your team.

It's also smart to have good relationships with your coaches and your parents. Your coaches are going to teach and guide you. They'll make the decisions about where you play, when you play, and how often you play. Your parents are going to support you. They're going to be paying for your uniform, driving you to practices, taking you to games, offering advice, and helping you whenever you need help. Your coaches and parents are actually part of your overall team, aren't they? In a team sport, they are just as important as your teammates.

Remember that building relationships and making friends don't happen overnight. You have to work at it constantly. Also, it takes time for people to get to know you and for you to get to know them. So it would be smart to start right away, wouldn't it?

Your Teammates

Many players feel that they need to make friends with only one or two of their teammates. A couple of kids to hang around with are enough, they think. But that's not very smart. Rudy tried to make friends with everybody. At first, some of the players really responded well to his friendliness. Others, however, did not. They were quiet.

But when Rudy finally got to dress for the last game of the season, he was surprised to find that many of the people who had not initially said too much to him were the very players who stood up for him when it counted the most. Rudy had earned their respect. He was not just their teammate. He really had become their friend.

How did Rudy build all those friendships? Well, over time, he followed these three simple rules:

1. Be Trustworthy

People want to be able to trust their friends. But trust doesn't come easy, it has to be earned. And how do you earn another person's trust? Well, for one thing, you have to tell the truth. So be honest, be sincere, and don't lie.

You also have to be dependable. You have to be a person that a friend can depend on. If you tell somebody that you're going to do something, then you better do it. If you tell someone that you're going to be at a certain place at a certain time, then you better be at that place at that time.

If you're a trustworthy person, then you also give your best effort when you're on the field of play. Your teammates need to trust that you will execute your particular role when you're in the game, that you will do your best, and that you will not give up. So you should try to be a leader and set an example. If you are always doing the best you can, if you always work hard and give it everything you've got, then you will earn the trust and respect of your teammates.

2. Be Unselfish

Have you ever heard anybody call a person a "one-man team"? Well, sure you have. But the worst thing a person can be in a team sport is a one-man team.

People who try to do it all are viewed as selfish. And selfish people don't have many friends.

But friends share things with each other. At home, they share stories, jokes, games, movies, and more. On a sports team, they share the ball. In basketball, instead of taking a shot yourself, you should throw the ball to the open person. In soccer, if one of your teammates is open in front of the net, you should pass it over to him so the team will have a better chance of scoring a goal. The best players give up the ball. They are more givers than takers. They also have the most friends.

3. Be Helpful

The greatness of a person is not how the person becomes great, but how the person makes others great. Real athletes understand that. They understand that it's not only about them, it's also about the team.

Isn't it true that friends help each other? Of course it is. True friends help each other solve their problems. They help each other get better. Instead of saying negative things, true friends are encouraging. For instance, if a teammate is trying hard but makes an error, rather than yelling or saying something negative, you should say: "Don't worry about it, buddy. You'll get the next one. Shake it off!"

If you're a starter on the team, you shouldn't look down on your teammates who don't start. You should help them get better so that they will be able to start one day. And you should do that even if it means that one day they'll take your position. Perhaps you're the best goalie in the league. But what about your teammate who wants to be a good goalie, and who always has to play behind you? You should teach that person everything you know. It will not only help the team if you get hurt, it will help you because you'll have a good friend.

On the other side of the coin, if you don't happen to be the best goalie on the team, you should encourage the starting goalie to be the best he or she can possibly be. Why? Because it will also help the team and you will also have a good friend.

Your Coach

How should you relate to your coach? Well, for starters, at the beginning of the season, go up and say hello. Introduce yourself. Your coach is there to help you, so get your coach comfortable giving you feedback. Let him or her know that you want to learn, that it's okay to tell you the least little thing if it will help your performance.

You should also think of your coach as a person. And because your coach is a human being, it is possible to build a good strong relationship with him or her, isn't it? Try to make the coach your friend—not on the same level as your teammates, but a friend nonetheless.

Remember that coaches can make mistakes just like all of us. They can also make poor decisions once in a while. So be sure not to put your coach on too high a pedestal. Rather, put your coach on a "respectful" level. That way, you will not overreact if your coach makes a mistake or a poor decision. If that happens, give your coach a break. Let it go. Remember, if you put your coach on too high a pedestal, you will inevitably be let down.

Sometimes, however, players do have serious problems with their coaches. The truth is that championships are often lost because members of a team have trouble with their coach. The players get angry. They say bad things and talk behind the coach's back. But that just makes it bad for everybody on the team. So what should you do if *you* have a problem with your coach?

The best thing to do is to talk to your coach in private. Ask for some time after practice. Tell your coach exactly how you feel. "Am I doing anything wrong?" you might ask. "Have I done anything to offend you? Can we talk about what happened the other day?"

You might be surprised at your coach's response. You might hear something that never occurred to you. If you are told specifically that he or she thinks you're doing something wrong, try not to take it too personally. Ask how you can get better.

Usually, a conversation like this will clear the air and make things a lot better. Sometimes, though, things don't get better. What do you do then?

Well, you might think about mentioning it to your parents.

Your Parents

One time when Rudy was playing Little League baseball, he got very upset because his coach yelled at him. And when Rudy got home, he told his mom and dad that he wanted to quit the team.

"But, Rudy," his dad said, "if you quit every time somebody yells at you, you're never going to finish anything."

"But that coach is a jerk! He's mean!"

"Does he yell at the other players?" asked Rudy's mom.

"Yes."

"Well then, he's not really singling you out if he yells at everybody. Do you think the other kids are going to quit?"

"I don't know," said Rudy.

"Listen, Son," said Rudy's dad, "it's not really about you. Your coach is not mad at you. He's mad at himself. He's the guy with the problem. Not you. You have to understand that."

"You think so?" asked Rudy.

"Yes," responded his mom.

"Absolutely," said his dad. "If you hang in there and don't quit, you're going to be a better person for it. You signed up and committed to play baseball for the season. And it should take more than a coach yelling for you to not fulfill that commitment, right?"

"I guess so," said Rudy.

"Tell you what," said Rudy's dad, "you keep going to practice and let's see what happens. Maybe it'll get better. If it doesn't, let me know. Maybe, then we can have a polite conversation with your coach."

Things eventually got better with that coach. Rudy finished the season and really had a good time. In the end, he was glad he didn't quit the team.

From that experience, Rudy learned that his parents were really there to help him. He would often go and talk to them when he had a problem. And they always listened and gave him advice.

Rudy was lucky, he never really had any big problems with his mom or dad. But some kids aren't so lucky. Some have a parent who wants them to play a certain sport that they really don't want to play. So what do you do if you have a problem like that? Well, you should start the same way you do when you have a problem with your coach. You should talk to your parents.

Be sincere and be polite, but ask this question: "Dad, do you really want me to play football *for me*? Or do you really want me to play football *for you*?" And then listen to your father. See what he has to say. If he says that he wants you to play football because he played football, you should just tell him that it's not your kind of sport and that you really don't want to play it.

But if your dad says, "I want you to play football because I want you to get involved in something," then that changes everything. Then you might respond by saying, "Okay, Dad. I understand. But I don't like football. Can we find something else for me to get involved in?" Your father will probably say, "Sure." And then he'll help you pick something that you like better.

Whenever you have a problem with your parents, the very best thing you can do is sit down and talk with them about it.

That's called communication. And communication is very, very important in having good relationships with people.

Remember that your relationship with your parents is probably the most important relationship you can have with anybody—especially at your age. If your parents sometimes make you mad, you can't quit loving them. You should tell them how you feel and try to work things out with them.

As a matter of fact, that's what you should try to do with all of your friends. If you do, you will have long-lasting relationships and lots of friends.

Things to Remember

4/Building Relationships and Making Friends

- On teams, people have to rely on each other to get things done. You can't do everything yourself.
- True friends want to help you succeed.
- Building relationships and making friends don't happen overnight. You have to constantly work at it.
- Make friends with all your teammates.
- In building friendships, follow these three simple rules:
  1. Be Trustworthy
  2. Be Unselfish
  3. Be Helpful
- Trust doesn't come easily. It has to be earned.
- Give your best effort when you're on the field of play.
- Don't be a one-man team.
- The greatness of a person is not how the person becomes great, but how the person makes others great.
- Coaches are human beings too. They can make mistakes. Don't put them on too high a pedestal. Put them on a "respectful" level.
- If you have a problem with your coach, ask for some time after practice. Tell your coach exactly how you feel.
- If your parents make you mad sometimes, you can't quit loving them.
- Remember that your parents are on your team. They are there to help you. So respect them and communicate with them.
- Communication is key to having good relationships with people.

In this lifetime, you don't have to
prove anything to anybody except yourself.

Chapter 5
Being True to Yourself

There was a moment in Rudy's journey when he came very close to giving up. It was just prior to the last practice before his last home game at Notre Dame. When Rudy walked up to the bulletin board to see if his name was on the list of players who could dress for the game, he knew this was his last chance. If his name was not on that list, he would not be able to achieve his dream of playing football for Notre Dame. It was a tense moment for Rudy. When he went up to the bulletin board, he was surrounded by his teammates. He scrolled his finger down the list. But his name was not there.

"Sorry, man," said a couple of the guys. "Sorry."

But Rudy really didn't hear them. He was angry, very angry—and he stalked off in a huff.

"I should have listened to all those people who told me I'd never make it," Rudy thought to himself. "I worked hard for this. That darn coach! He should have put me on the list. Why did I even try? Why? The heck with everybody. I'm not going to that last practice. I quit!"

But then Rudy ran into the janitor. "What are you doing here?" asked Fortune. "Don't you have practice."

"Not anymore. I quit!" said Rudy.

"Well, since when are you the quitting kind?" he responded.

"I don't know. I just don't see the point anymore."

"So you didn't make the dress list. There are greater tragedies in the world."

"I wanted to run out of that tunnel to prove to everybody that—"

And then Fortune interrupted Rudy. "Prove what?" he asked.

"That I was somebody," said Rudy dejectedly.

And then Fortune really let Rudy have it.

"Rudy, you're five feet nothing. A hundred and nothing. You have hardly a speck of athletic ability. And you hung in with the best college football team in the land *for two years*. And you're also going to walk out of here with a degree from the University of Notre Dame. In this lifetime, you don't have to prove anything to anybody except yourself. And after what you've gone through, if you haven't done that by now, it'll never happen."

Those words really made Rudy stop and think.

Fortune then told Rudy to go back to practice. He told him if he walked out now, he would always regret letting other people get the best of him.

Never Compromise Your Character

After that conversation, Rudy's attitude changed. He realized that just because he hadn't achieved his dream, just because he didn't get something he felt he deserved, it didn't mean that there was somebody to blame. It didn't mean that he should blame the coach, or the other players, or anybody else. That was just the way things were. There was nobody to blame.

Rudy then asked himself what was really, truly important to him. And the answer surprised him.

It would have been great to dress, he thought, to run through the tunnel with his teammates, but Fortune was right. It *wasn't* the end of the world. What really meant something to him was that he gave it his all. And he had been a good person in the process. He always told the truth. He stuck with his commitment. He learned along the way. He worked hard. He cared about his teammates. He earned their trust, wasn't selfish, and tried to help them whenever he could. Rudy had done his best and, while doing it, he had put his whole heart into it. He took great pride in the fact that he never compromised his character. And, by God, that really meant something!

At this point in his journey, Rudy Ruettiger had not achieved his dream. But he had won in life. And if *you* do the same thing Rudy did, you will win in life, too. With Rudy's kind of attitude, you will be successful sooner or later because *everybody* who has that kind of attitude and that kind of character succeeds in the long run.

And don't forget that, at the end of your journey, it really doesn't matter much what other people think of you. What matters most is what you think of yourself.

Because Rudy believed in himself, he decided to go back to practice. He was late in getting there—and all the players were already on the field going through their drills.

When Rudy came out onto the field, his teammates were very surprised. "Hey," one of them said in amazement, "it's Rudy."

Then the guys started applauding for him. And when he got back into the huddle, his friends patted him on the back and wrapped their arms around him. They were glad to see him. And they were proud of him.

<u>Never Quit</u>

We all know Rudy eventually became the most famous football player from the University of Notre Dame. But it wasn't because he was a great athlete. And it wasn't because he was a better person than anybody else. It was because on the day he went back to practice, he displayed a very important quality. On that day, Rudy showed spirit. He never quit—even when things looked hopeless.

Have you ever thought about what it really means to quit?

Quitting means going away because you don't want to confront a tough situation. It means giving up on a commitment, or giving up on your friends or, worse yet, giving up on yourself. It means giving in to your fears.

Everybody knows it takes courage not to give up. It takes courage to confront your fears when you're afraid, or worried, or depressed. If you start quitting when you're young, then you are going to do more quitting when you get older. And then the odds are that you'll never be successful in anything—because every time the going gets tough, you'll give up and go home.

But if you don't give up when you're young, then you will eventually achieve a lot of things. People will admire and remember you for it. And if they ever get the opportunity, they will go out of their way to help you. That's what happened to Rudy.

When he didn't make the dress roster, Rudy's teammates saw that he was very disappointed—and they felt he had every reason to give up and walk away. Actually, that's what they thought he would do. But when Rudy strode back onto the practice field to take his licks like everybody else—even though he knew he was not going to realize his dream—the other players were really impressed. And they decided to try and help him.

After practice, several went to the head coach and laid their jerseys on his desk. "Coach, I want Rudy to dress in my place," they said. "He deserves it."

"Me, too, Coach. I want Rudy to dress in *my* place," they said.

"Coach, this is for Rudy."

"For Rudy, Coach."

If Rudy had not gone back to practice, if he had said "the heck with everybody" and just walked away—then he would never have achieved his dream. That's because the players would never have gone to the coach and offered to give up their places on the roster so that their friend could play. Because Rudy did not give up on his teammates, his teammates did not give up on him.

Have Fun and Enjoy the Journey

Before Rudy was accepted into Notre Dame, Father Cavanaugh, the former president of the university, told him that he had done a great job chasing down his dream.

"I don't care what kind of a job I did," replied Rudy. "If it doesn't produce results, it doesn't mean anything."

Father Cavanaugh paused for a moment, looked at Rudy, and said, "I think you'll discover that it will."

In the years after graduating from Notre Dame, Rudy came to realize that Father Cavanaugh had been right. The journey to his dream had lasted three years. The things he experienced, the lessons he learned, the fun he had, the relationships he developed, and the friends he made—all these memories and friendships were going to last a lifetime.

That's the way it is when you're playing sports. Every year, your journey will last for a whole season. There are things to learn, relationships to be developed, friends to be made, and a lot of fun to be had. So you should enjoy yourself while you're out there, shouldn't you? You should enjoy the journey and have as much fun as you can. If you don't, you're only cheating yourself and your teammates.

After the other players went to the head coach and offered to give up their jerseys to let their little buddy play, the coach added Rudy to the roster. He got to dress and run through the tunnel and onto the field with the other players. But Rudy didn't get into the game until the last quarter, when there were only twenty-seven seconds left on the clock. So it was a three-year journey with a "result" that lasted only twenty-seven seconds. When Rudy began to think about that, he realized that the journey was just as important as the dream.

During those final twenty-seven seconds, Rudy participated in two plays. The first was a kickoff, and he basically just ran down the field. When the second play began, there were only seven seconds left on the clock. Rudy lined up on the defensive line with his teammates. He looked only half the size of the offensive player standing next to him. "He's so little!" one of his friends yelled.

When the ball was snapped, Rudy wheeled around the offensive player, got into the backfield, and tackled the quarterback just as time expired.

The crowd stood and cheered. Tens of thousands of people chanted, "RU-DY! RU-DY! RU-DY!" His parents cried. His coaches smiled. And Rudy's teammates lifted him onto their shoulders and carried him off the field. In the many years since, no other football player has ever been carried off the field at Notre Dame.

The little guy, Rudy Ruettiger, who was "too small," who had "no chance," who was told to "get another dream"—was on top of the world, looked-up to, and cheered by thousands. It was *better* than *anything* he had *ever* dreamed of. It was one of the greatest moments in Rudy's life.

That is the power of a dream.

Things to Remember

5/Being True to Yourself

- Just because you don't get something you feel you deserve doesn't mean that there is somebody to blame.
- Ask yourself what is really, truly important to you.
- At the end of your journey, it really doesn't matter much what other people think of you. What matters most is what you think of yourself.
- Never compromise your character.
- Quitting means going away because you don't want to confront a tough situation. It means giving up on a commitment, or giving up on your friends or, worse yet, giving up on yourself. It means giving into your fears.
- Show spirit by never quitting—even when things look hopeless.
- It takes courage to confront your fears when you're afraid, or worried, or depressed.
- If you quit when you're young, then you are going to quit when you get older.
- People will admire you if you don't give up. And if they get the opportunity, they will go out of their way to help you.
- The kind of job you do, the way you conduct yourself, *does* mean something. It *does* matter.
- Enjoy the journey and have as much fun as you can.

Part II

Parents

You be the adult.
Let the kids be kids.

Chapter 6
Being Informed and Involved

As a parent, you want the best for your children. You want them to be well-rounded, to interact properly with other children, to learn different things, and to develop a foundation of good character.

Youth sports can be a wonderful place for all that to take place. In a well-run youth sports program, kids are involved in an organized activity where their energy is directed in a positive way. It's also a place where they may learn discipline, patience, how to be part of a team, and other useful life lessons.

Many parents enroll their kids in a sports program. Some use it as a convenient babysitting service. Some watch what's going on from a distance. And most go to the games and cheer on the team. But all parents should be informed about everything that is happening to their child in a youth sports program. And they should be involved in every key decision.

As children grow, they need guidance and direction. They need to be told what to do, while at the same time being allowed to choose their own paths. A parent's job isn't easy. It's a delicate balance of listening and talking, of telling and selling, of love and discipline.

See Life through Your Child's Eyes

Do you remember what it was like to be a kid? Birthdays with cake, ice cream, and presents. Doing things with your pals, like going to movies, to sleepovers, or just goofing around. The best times were carefree and happy-go-lucky, weren't they? Most adults would agree that their fondest memories of childhood revolve around having fun.

Well, the same is true of kids today—especially those involved in youth sports. Surveys consistently indicate that more than nine out of ten kids state that their top reason for joining a sports team is "to have fun." As a parent, *you* are the one who want them to learn teamwork, discipline, and all these other important things. But from *their* point of view, it's all about having a good time with their pals.

Some parents tend to forget that their children are not adults. They might come home from work after a hard day dealing with cranky bosses or coworkers and have a tough time changing their mindset to deal with that little person who wants to immediately go outside and kick the ball or play catch. The same thing can happen during a youth sporting event, when parents on the sidelines sometimes forget that the game they're watching is being played by *children*—not by other grown-ups.

A child's view of life, however, is very different from an adult's view. For instance, during a close soccer game with only a couple of minutes left to play, most parents are thinking about scoring a goal. But many of the kids might only be thinking about ending the game so they can run through the tunnel and eat the after-game snacks. And the younger the kids are, the greater the odds that they don't have any idea that it's a close game, let alone what the score is.

Another example might be when a child gets fouled by a member of the opposing team. A parent sitting in the stands could become angry, because they assume that it was done on purpose. But their child might not be angry at all. As a matter of fact, they might not even know what the infraction was all about. Or, if they do, they might just think that the other kid made a mistake, which can happen to anybody—and they're probably already looking toward taking a free kick (or a free throw, etc.).

Some parents take youth sports to the extreme and try to relive their own childhoods through their kids. We all know the type. "I want Johnny to play football, because I played football," or "I want Sally to swim, because I was a swimmer." Well, these parents see their children's lives only through their own eyes. They don't pause to think about how their kids see things.

The aspirations these parents have for their children do not coincide with their children's aspirations. In such cases, even though parents might not be aware of it, their children probably feel forced into doing something they don't really want to do. And when children believe they're being forced into something, it always feels more like punishment than fun.

As a parent, do you have the patience and foresight to stop and ask yourself, "What is my child thinking at this moment? How is my child seeing this situation?" If you do, you can rest assured that both you and your child will gain a great deal more out of your experience with youth sports than you ever thought possible.

Remember to be the adult. Let the kids be kids.

Help Your Child Find a Dream

One of the greatest things about kids is their imaginations. To kids, anything is possible. They can go anywhere. They can do anything. They can be anybody they want to be. Unless, of course, an adult says to them, "Don't be ridiculous," or "Get serious," or "That's not possible," or "Forget it, you don't have a chance."

As a good parent, you simply cannot be one of those adults who kill a kid's dream. Rather, you should fan the fire of your child's imagination. Encourage him or her to think of all things possible. Help your child find a dream. Why? Because dreams are good things. They make life exciting. They give kids something to strive for. They are fun. And dreams come as naturally to children as flying does to birds.

So how do you help your children develop a dream? The first step is to expose them to a lot of different things—new things they've not yet tried, things that spark their imaginations. If you haven't already done so, take them to a soccer game, a volleyball match, a swim meet, and other sporting events.

Remember that children will react differently to various stimuli. Some things they'll like, some things they won't. And obviously, their reactions have a lot to do with their personalities. While some kids are introverted and shy, others are outgoing and talkative. Where do your children fall? If you don't know, you need to find out. You should search for your children's true personalities and look for their natural tendencies. In order to do that, you must sit back and watch closely.

Observe their reactions. Notice their body language. Do their eyes start to wander at a baseball game? Are they bored during a volleyball match? Are they mesmerized by the skating during a hockey game? Watch for the moment when they come alive. Often, something that interests them will coincide with their personalities. An introspective kid might like baseball. An especially physical one might get excited about hockey.

Watch for that sparkle in your child's eyes, for the passion, for the unusual interest. When you see it, jump on it. Start a conversation. "This looks fun, doesn't it? What do you like about it?"

Make eye contact with your children. Get them to talk. And then listen to what they have to say. If your child says, "That really looks like fun. I want to do that," then you're starting to make progress.

If, a few days later, your child starts watching the sport on television and then comes and says, "Mom, I want to be Mia Hamm," then you're there. *That* is a dream.

And what are you going to do at that point? Are you going to say, "You can't be Mia Hamm"? Or are you going to say, "Okay, great! Let's go get a ball. Then we'll sign you up in a soccer league."

Remember, never ever shut down your child's "want to." Get your children involved in things that interest them. Let *them* be the drivers of their own activities. Let them dream.

Guide and Focus

Once you are dialed into your children's interests and dreams, you have the opportunity to open up a whole new world to them. And you can be sure that nobody else will do it for them unless you, as their parent, take the lead.

So sit your child down and have a conversation. You might begin by saying something like, "Okay, if you 'want to' be Mia

Hamm, you're going to 'have to' do some things." And then rattle off a couple of examples.

At this point, it's a good idea to start using plural pronouns so your child understands that he or she is not in it alone. "*We* have to learn all about soccer. *We* have to start practicing. *We* have to get in a soccer league."

If there's excitement and enthusiasm in your voice, then you can be sure your child will start to get excited and enthusiastic. "Okay, let's make a list," you might say next. "In order to learn about soccer, why don't we start by reading a book about the sport? Then we can talk to some people who've been playing it for a while. What do you think?"

"Yeah, Mom, that sounds great. Terry's dad is a coach. Maybe we can talk to him."

"Good idea. That's number three. We'll talk to Terry's dad."

Now you're in the beginning stages of putting together a plan designed to guide and focus your child toward making the dream happen.

Here are a few key elements that should go into the plan:

1. Involve your child in the planning process.

2. Write things down.

3. Make the goals realistic, achievable, and measurable.

4. Be sure to follow through. Take your child to the bookstore or library and pick out a few books to read. Call Terry's dad and set up a meeting.

Remember, you can't leave it all up to your child to follow through. Kids have short attention spans. They will get wrapped up in what they're doing at the moment and will forget about the list of "have to's." It's up to you to remind them.

You are their parent. If you don't focus and guide your children, who will?

Tips for Parents

6/Being Informed and Involved

- As your children grow, they need to be told what to do, while at the same time, allowed to choose their own paths.

- Remember what it was like to be a kid.

- A child's view of life is very different from an adult's view. See life through your child's eyes.

- When children believe they are being forced to do something, it feels more like punishment than fun.

- Remember to be the adult. Let the kids be kids.

- Encourage your child to dream.

- Expose your children to a variety of new things—things that spark their imaginations.

- Search for your child's true personality. Look for his or her natural tendencies.

- Once you are dialed into your children's interests, you have the opportunity to open up a whole new world to them.

- Sit down and have a conversation with your child.

- Put a plan together that is designed to focus and guide your child toward making their dream happen.

- Key elements of the plan should be:

  1. Involve your child in the planning process.

  2. Write things down.

  3. Make the goals realistic, achievable, and measurable.

  4. Follow through. Help your child implement the plan.

Forget about keeping a report card. Forget about winning and losing.
In youth sports, every child gets an A. Every child is a winner.

Chapter 7

Connecting with Your Child During the Season

As children grow and develop, their personal self-image is based largely on what they hear other people say to them—and *about* them. Clearly, a child's parents have the most impact in this area. If kids hear kind words from Mom and Dad, if they hear positive comments, then they will have higher self-esteem and more self-confidence.

Studies in psychology confirm that children who have poor self-images haven't yet received enough positive attention and feedback. So, as parents, you have the opportunity to lay the foundation of a positive self-image for your child. Youth sports can be a great avenue to make that happen. But in order to do so, you must have a positive, ongoing relationship with your children. You must be "connected" to them during the entire season—from beginning to end.

Teach Commitment

One Saturday afternoon, Jimmy's father took him to a kid's basketball game. The next day, the boy wanted to join a team and get into the game. So Jimmy's parents signed him up and took him to the first team meeting, where he met the coach and the other players—and you could just see the excitement in Jimmy's eyes. But after the first practice, he came home and said, "Daddy, I don't want to play basketball anymore."

It's a familiar occurrence. A child goes to practice, doesn't enjoy the experience for one reason or another, comes home, and wants to quit right then and there. How parents handle this situation can leave a long-lasting impression on their child.

First of all, you should consider what is really going on in your child's mind. What is Jimmy really afraid of? Perhaps he's worried that he might not have the talent or athletic skill to keep up with the other boys. Maybe he thinks if he doesn't have what it takes, he will be humiliated or rejected. Could it be that he's simply afraid to fail? That's not only a normal reaction for a child trying out a new sport for the first time, it can also be a very scary thing for a kid to go through.

After you've considered what your child is thinking, sit him down and talk him through it. Find out what happened in practice. Reassure him that what he's feeling is perfectly normal. In fact, most of the other kids are probably feeling exactly the same way. Tell him a story about how you felt when you were in a similar situation—and how everything turned out okay. And then talk to him about commitment, about not quitting too early.

"Well, Jimmy," you might say, "we committed to play basketball for this season. We can't quit after the first practice, or any practice. We've got to see it through. I'm sure things will get better as you go along."

As a parent, however, you have to do more than just reassure your child. You should do what you can to help him feel more comfortable with the sport. Take some time at home, for instance, to work on basic skills. Go out to the driveway and practice dribbling the ball with your son. Once he starts to get the hang of it, praise him: "That's great, Jimmy. You're doing very well. I'll bet that's as good as any of the other kids can do."

As your child gets better, call attention to his progress. Even the slightest bit of improvement, if mentioned in the correct manner, can make a profound impression on a kid: "Wow, Jimmy. Last week you couldn't shoot the ball that well. Look how you've improved. I can't wait to see what you'll be able to do next week."

It really doesn't take a lot of time or effort for a parent to interact with their child in this manner. A child will be happy to have ten or fifteen minutes of one-on-one time with Mom or Dad. That seems like a brief period of time for an adult, but for a young child with a short attention span, it can be more than enough time to have a very positive impact.

Spending one-on-one time with your kids not only helps develop their athletic skills, it helps to develop a positive self-image. It's also a tangible way to demonstrate to your children that you care about them. And to a child, a parent's time is the most valuable thing in the world.

So spend some time with your child talking about commitment. If you don't, then your kids may get in the habit of never finishing anything they start. They may grow into adults who never get anything done, who never achieve any kind of success.

Be Positive and Encouraging

All children have an innate desire to please their parents. The younger the child, the more pronounced the desire. Some sports psychologists even believe that before, during, and after a game, the foremost thing in a child's mind is to do whatever it takes to achieve parental approval. Whether or not this is at the top of a kid's thoughts, or buried somewhere in his or her subconscious, it is clearly there somewhere. So on game day, every parent should be prepared on a moment's notice to say a few positive and encouraging words to their child.

Before a game, keep an eye on your child. Watch her body language and facial expressions. Does she seem anxious and apprehensive—or excited and enthusiastic? Her mood will guide your comments. Either way, anything you say should be upbeat. Be sure not to make the mistake of putting pressure on your child. Don't even think about winning or losing. Talk about having fun and enjoying the time with friends and teammates. Mention the snacks at the end of the game or something similar. Keep the atmosphere light and enjoyable.

During a game, it's almost always a good idea for parents to be at their children's games to support and cheer them on. Sit back and observe while the game is going on. If your child looks over at you and makes eye contact, flash her a smile. While the action is taking place, it's better not to yell out instructions. Kids need to explore on their own, to make mistakes on their own, and to learn on their own. Let them experience the joy in winning and the disappointment in losing—the excitement of making a good play and the frustration of making an error. Remember, the game is for your child, not you.

After a game, be there to support your child. But be careful not to be too excited when the team wins or too depressed when the team loses. Keep an even keel and stay positive. Kids are quick to pick up on anything negative you might say. It's a good idea to start a conversation with your child by asking questions. "Did you have fun?" "What part did you like the best?" "Did you feel good in your uniform?" If she's feeling down because she had a poor game, give her some breathing room. Let her talk it out—or let her be quiet, if that's what she wants.

But after a while, find something in her performance to praise. "I really like the way you hustled on and off the field." "I thought it was great when you gave a high five to Jessica after she scored that goal." "I saw that pass you made in the first half. It was terrific." If your child responds by saying, "But, Dad, I let them get by me and they scored that goal,"— you can remind her that everybody gets scored on now and then. Say to her, "You have to put it behind you and plan on stopping them the next time." Just remember to be as positive as you possibly can.

After a game, every kid wants to be praised. Some parents like to keep a "report card" on every game. Normally, kids don't feel good about that. They have enough pressure about grades in school. So forget about keeping a report card. Forget about winning and losing. In youth sports, every child gets an A. Every child is a winner.

During the season, of course, there will be times when you'll have to correct your child. And coming up with positive and encouraging things to say can be somewhat challenging. But you definitely need to say something to them if they tell a lie, or start to complain too much, or have a pity party with the other kids, and so on. While it is usually best to address the problem right away, you can still speak calmly. You can start slowly and be constructive without being intimidating. Steer your children gently. Avoid hammering them. But don't avoid talking to them when necessary.

Other times during the season, you may need to provide some basic guidance. For instance, suppose your son comes home and says, "Mom, I think I'd like to try to be a pitcher. I think I could do a good job." But then you find out he hasn't mentioned his desire to the coach, because he's too shy. What do you do as a parent? Do you call the coach and mention it yourself? That's one way to do it. A better way might be to encourage your son to say something to the coach himself. "Why don't you get to practice early and tell your coach you'd like to give pitching a try? You have a good arm. He might think it's a good idea."

The point here is not to do everything for your child. Suggest, advise, encourage—but don't order or take charge. Teach your children to do things for themselves. In doing so, you'll be giving them an edge in life. How you treat them when they're young will determine how they act when they're adults. What you say to them at the age of six will be with them when they're sixty. So seize every opportunity to smother your kids with encouragement and positive feedback.

Reevaluate at Season's End

After the last game has been played, after the team party, take some time to speak with your child about the season as a whole.

"Well, Jimmy, what did you think about your first year of basketball?"

"It was fun, Dad."

Point out to him what he learned. You might mention skills like dribbling, passing, or shooting, working on plays with his teammates, and so on. Most children delight in mastering an athletic skill. But sometimes it's up to the parents to remind them of how much they've accomplished. If Jimmy really believes he's done well, it might encourage him to play another season.

At this point, you might also remind him that after the first practice, he wanted to quit. Remind him again about why not quitting is important. "Look how much fun you had. Look how much you learned. Look at all the new friends you made. Aren't you glad you didn't quit after the first practice?" Tell him that you're proud of him for not quitting after that first practice—and make sure he realizes that it was a *very* good decision.

The end of the season is also the time to take a reality check on your child's "want to." Ask her whether she still wants to play soccer. She might say, "Absolutely, Dad. I still want to be Mia Hamm." Or she might surprise you and announce that she wants to give volleyball a try. Now, it's okay to make that change. She has fulfilled her commitment and now it's time to make a new decision. "Okay, sweetheart. Let's give volleyball a try."

Also speak with your child about success and what it really means. Is success winning every game you play? Is it winning the league championship? If that's the case, there are going to be a lot of kids who won't be happy after the season is over because almost nobody wins every game, and only one team can win the championship.

Maybe success means something other than winning games. Ask your child, "Did you learn something?" "Did you do the best you could?" "Did you make some new friends?" "Did you enjoy yourself?" "Did you have fun?" "Are you happy you played?" "Do you want to do it again?" If the answers to all these questions are "yes"—then maybe your child had a successful season.

After you've talked to your child about the season, ask yourself if you, as a parent, had a successful season. Did you create an environment for your child that was "can do," positive, and encouraging? Did your child learn and grow? Is your child happy and self-confident. Does he or she have a positive self-image? Are *you* happy with your efforts? Are you proud of your child? If you can answer "yes" to these questions, then chances are you also had a successful season.

Tips for Parents

7/Connecting with Your Child during the Season

- You have the opportunity to lay the foundation of a positive self-image for your child.

- You must have a positive, ongoing relationship with your child during the season.

- Fear of failure is a normal reaction for a child trying a new sport for the first time.

- Reassure your child. Talk about commitment and not quitting too early.

- Take some time at home to work on basic athletic skills with your child.

- Call attention to the slightest bit of progress and improvement.

- Spending one-on-one time with your children helps them develop positive self-images.

- To a child, a parent's time is the most valuable thing in the world.

- Before a game, talk about having fun and enjoying the time with friends and teammates.

- Go to the kids' games. Listen, observe, support, and cheer. But don't yell out instructions.

- After a game, ask some easy questions. Give your child some space. Find something to praise.

- When called for, correct your child right away. But be constructive rather than intimidating.

- After the last game, sit down and talk about the season.

- Ask your child whether he or she wants to continue in the same sport—or try something else next season.

- Discuss what success really means.

When you lose your cool, you embarrass your child.
And remember, one unfortunate act done in a moment
of rage can last a lifetime in your child's mind.

Chapter 8
Personal Conduct

In neighborhoods all across the country, summer weekends are dominated by gatherings of adults and children at sporting events. Often it's the only time people really get together on a regular basis with those outside their immediate families or next-door neighborhood clique. So sporting events, from a social standpoint, tend to be much more important than one might first think. What would it be like if, at these gatherings, everybody treated everybody else with discourtesy and disrespect? What if everybody wanted to have things their way all the time? What if there was no good sportsmanship at any youth sporting event?

Sounds ridiculous, doesn't it? But there is one group of people who can really control behavior at a kids' game—the parents of the kids. Didn't you sign up your child for a sports program so that he or she could interact with other children? So your child could learn discipline, patience, good sportsmanship, and how to be part of a team? Well, as the parents behave, so behave the children. Therefore, a parent's conduct at a kid's game is *crucial* to the proper development of their children. Crucial!

The importance of personal conduct among adults at youth sporting events goes beyond good manners and politeness. It has a direct bearing on decent relations among human beings—not to mention the proper behavioral development of children.

Demonstrate Personal Excellence

The impact parents have on kids is huge—much bigger than even most parents realize. Kids are always watching their parents. They notice how their father shakes hands with another parent, how their mother chats with other moms, how both parents interact with the coach, and virtually everything else they do. Behaviors, mannerisms, language, and various elements of character are emulated and become part of the personality of the youngster.

Of course, all this is fundamental sociology, basic human nature. But how many parents really think about such things when they are in the stands of their son's basketball game or their daughter's softball game? While the potential impact of the parents' personal behavior on their child cannot be expected to be foremost in their thoughts, it should always be in the back of their minds.

The truth is that *any* negative behavior during a kid's game can be harmful. Too many parents, however, continually exhibit poor conduct while in the stands. Based on experience, here are a few things that should *not* be done:

Don't bark out instructions to your child.

Don't give your child's coach a hard time.

Don't scream at the officials.

Don't ridicule, taunt, or bad-mouth opposing players or coaches.

Don't get in verbal or physical altercations with anybody.

Don't blame anybody else for a loss.

Wouldn't it be better if parents demonstrated personal excellence where their children were involved? Actually, some youth leagues demand that parents behave. If they do not, they have to remove both themselves and their kids from the league.

Responsible people who run youth leagues recommend the following points as proper behavior for parents in the stands. If applied, these guidelines can help parents become role models in personal conduct.

Cheer for your child and for the members of your child's team.

Be positive in your remarks to everybody.

Remain quiet if an official makes a controversial call. Let the coaches handle it.

Smile and act with kindness and courtesy toward everybody.

Realize that, in the long run, winning or losing a kid's game is not really a big deal.

Focus on what's best for the children.

Treat the Coach with Respect

Most youth sports coaches are volunteers. Some have experience in the sport they're coaching, but many do not. They are simply parents who have a kid on the team and want to be involved. From this standpoint, they are very much like every other parent. So why not help them out? Why not work with them? Why not treat them with the respect and dignity that you would want to receive from other parents if you were walking in their shoes?

The beginning of a season can be a daunting time for a coach. Trying to get to know the kids, their personalities and talents, and the level of their skills can take quite a bit of time. It's not very realistic to expect the coach to come up to you right off the bat to speak about your child. That's why *you* should take the initiative.

At an appropriate time (perhaps after practice), go up and talk to the coach. Ask how you can be of help to the team. Let the coach know early on that you'd like to form an alliance. Ask him or her to keep an eye on your child. "If there are any concerns, please call me," you might say, "and please let me know what I can do to help my daughter be a better athlete or be more effective for the team."

Most youth coaches will appreciate the gesture. It's always good to know that the parents of the kids they're coaching are decent people who want to help. It makes the time they invest seem more worthwhile.

Over the course of the season, it's possible that you or your child might have some kind of misunderstanding with the coach. What happens, for instance, if your son or daughter comes home after a practice and complains about something the coach said or did? The first thing to remember is not to overreact. Often a kid's perception of what an adult does is very different from what is really going on in the adult's mind. Ask your child for some details. Find out if there is really a serious problem or not. If there isn't, tell your child to remember that the coach is a person just like the rest of us. He or she can make mistakes—and perhaps it *was* just a mistake. Make sure that your child doesn't get into the habit of saying negative things about the coach to the other kids. Complaining or having pity parties cannot only be detrimental to a team, it can also become a bad habit.

If, after talking to your child, you find that there really may be a serious problem with the coach, reassure your child that everything will be all right—that he or she should not worry about it, and should think about having fun the next time out. Then it would be a good idea to call the coach on the phone and describe what your child has said. Usually, everything can be cleared up with one conversation. If not, and if it is a serious problem (which is very infrequent), check with your league president to find out what options you might have for further action. It also might be a good idea to speak with other parents on the team to see if anyone else is experiencing a similar problem.

What happens if the coach does something during a game that you disagree with? The best thing to do is to bite your tongue and just keep quiet. Remember that people have different perspectives, different views, different opinions on strategy. If it's a small thing, just let it go.

However, if it's a major thing, like not letting your child play as much as the other children, then it's wise to say something *after* the game, in private, out of earshot of the other parents and kids. A phone call that evening or the next day might be appropriate.

Most coaches are usually receptive to cordial, respectful discussions. And any misunderstandings are frequently worked out immediately. The worst thing a parent can do is sit around and stew about something that might not be a big deal. Doing so often spirals into an out-of-control mindset where people can begin to imagine all sorts of unrealistic things. Remember, when in doubt, don't talk behind the coach's back—talk directly to the coach.

A youth sports coach is almost always a decent person who just wants to help out. So build a relationship with him or her. Establish a high level of trust. Give support and show respect. After all, this person is coaching, teaching, and guiding your child. There not much in life that's more important than that.

Channel Your Emotions

If there's anything that can bring out the emotion in a quiet, stoic father or a sweet, petite mother—it's a game where their children are involved. Many parents can find themselves barking out orders to their kids without even realizing what they're doing. Some can find themselves pacing back and forth, mumbling to themselves. Others end up pestering the coach to do this or to do that. And a few parents can absolutely "lose it"—even to the point of verbally and physically abusing officials, coaches, and other parents.

As a responsible parent, you have to be aware of how you're feeling when watching one of your child's games. You must channel your emotions so that you may set a good example and make the sporting event a positive experience. Remember that the kids are always watching. When you lose your cool, you embarrass your child.

Parents most often overreact when their children make a mistake on the field. The next time you're at a game and a child makes an error, glance over at that child's parents. You'll likely see some sort of response. The range of reactions can be anything from a frown to an expletive directed toward the field. If your child makes a mistake during the game, you should not let it get to you. Stay calm. Remember, they're just kids. They're going to make mistakes. That's how they learn.

The last thing you need to do is yell something from the stands like, "C'mon, Johnny, get your act together!" It upsets your child and makes you look intolerant. Besides, if you put your children on the defensive every time they commit an error, they'll be afraid to even try the next time the situation presents itself.

Another common reaction from a parent occurs when someone in the stands says something stupid. If a nonthinking parent, for instance, says something uncouth about your child, try to shake it off. Take yourself out of the situation. Get up and walk away. When you come back, find a different seat. The idea is to take yourself out of a situation where you might become upset and overreact in a public way that embarrasses or harms your child.

If you're an emotional person and have tendencies to say things you later regret, you might also think about taking some steps ahead of time to curb your passions. Look at yourself in the mirror before you go to the game. Remind yourself to be cool and calm. Ask your spouse or a friend to pinch you if you start getting out of control. Do whatever it takes to keep your emotions in check. Remember, one unfortunate act done in a moment of rage can last a lifetime in your child's mind.

When your child makes a mistake, it does not reflect directly on you. Don't be one of those sad parents who have low self-esteem and live life through their children. It helps nobody and hurts everybody—especially your children.

Tips for Parents
8/Personal Conduct

- One group of people who can really control behavior at a kid's game is the parents.

- A parent's conduct at a kid's game is *crucial* to the proper development of their children.

- Remember, your children are always watching. With time, they will pattern their lives after you.

- The potential impact of your behavior on your child should always be in the back of your mind.

- Always demonstrate personal excellence where your kids are involved.

- Remember, most coaches are simply parents who have a kid on the team and want to be involved. Treat them as you would want to be treated.

- When you disagree with the coach on small matters, just bite your tongue and let it go.

- If you disagree with the coach on a serious matter, first speak privately with the coach.

- As a responsible parent, you have to be aware of how you're feeling when watching one of your child's games.

- When you lose your cool, you embarrass your child.

- After your child makes an error during the game, don't let it get to you. Stay calm. Let them learn from their mistakes.

- Take some steps before the game to help channel your emotions.

- Don't be one of those sad parents who have low self-esteem and live life through their children.

Tell your children that it's not about "you," it's about "us."
It's not about "me," it's about "we."
And then walk your talk.

Chapter 9
Nurturing the Team Concept

Participation in youth sports brings a new level to the lives of most kids. For many, it is their first experience in a group setting other than school. But being part of a sports team goes beyond even school. For the first time, a child can experience a real sense of belonging. And feeling accepted into a peer group, as we all know, is a basic human need.

When children put on their team uniforms, they instantly well up with a sense of pride. You can often see it in their faces. And they look forward to the games not so much for the sport itself, but because of the camaraderie among their teammates.

Being part of a team teaches young people how to get along with one another. It helps them learn mutual respect, mutual responsibility, trust, and better communication. These, of course, are all priceless skills.

The opportunities for parents to nurture the team concept in their children are virtually endless. When those opportunities are used wisely, parents can provide their kids with an edge in dealing with people. They can give them a head start in life. The more they do so, the better—and the sooner the better.

Relationships

One of the many reasons cited by parents for involving their children in sports is to give them the chance to have relationships outside of normal school situations. With time, the kids become friends. They learn how to give and take, how to meld with a group and, with proper guidance, they learn that trust is the foundation of all relationships.

In a team sport environment, your children are in a situation where they just naturally start building relationships with other players and coaches. But you should also encourage them to connect with additional people. For instance, if your child wants to play hockey, and you don't know anything about hockey, then find someone who does. A friend at work or a next-door neighbor may be a hockey coach. Or there may be an older kid in the neighborhood who's been playing hockey for years. Call him up, talk to him, and ask him to speak with your child.

Finding someone to be a mentor, a tutor, or a private coach is a good idea. It not only helps your son or daughter learn more about the technical aspects of the sport they're engaged in, it also gives them the chance to cultivate a relationship with another adult or an older kid. And that creates an entirely new level of relationship-building for your child. It exposes them to more people, makes them more well-rounded. And who knows, a mentor might actually say the same thing to your child that you've been saying for a long time—which will give you more credibility in your child's eyes. That, in turn, will enhance your own relationship with your son or daughter.

Learning how to be with other people, and how to build relationships, is important in life. In this world, we can't do everything alone. We need relationships with others to help make our dreams come true, to comfort each other, and to live more full and rewarding lives. The sooner your children start to cultivate relationships, the better chance they will have to be both successful and happy in life.

Sometimes the friendships formed in youth leagues last a lifetime. And if you have a friend of your own that goes that far back, you know how priceless such a relationship can be.

Unselfishness

Often kids will want to quit a team because the coach won't let them play in a certain position all the time. They'll come home to their parents and complain, "I want to play shortstop, but the coach won't let me play it all the time. He lets Kerry play there a lot of the time and puts me at second base or in the outfield."

A smart parent will usually respond with one word: "So?"

That will force the child to give the real reason for the problem. And the child might say, "Well, I want to play there *all* the time! The coach won't let me, so I'm going to quit!"

At this point, a parent has the opportunity to impart a valuable lesson. "No. You can't quit the team. You're being selfish. You can't have your way all the time. Why shouldn't your teammates be able to play? As a matter of fact, I've seen Kerry play, and Kerry is a better shortstop than you are. *Kerry* at shortstop makes the team better. Did you ever think about that?"

Kids are naturally selfish. Everybody is. But youth sports can be a perfect forum for teaching them selflessness and consideration for others. Teams always function better when its members are unselfish—when they sacrifice their desires for the betterment of the team as a whole. In team sports, kids not only hear the lesson from the parent or coach, they actually see it work with their own eyes in practices or in games. And that's when they really start to learn.

Parents can and should encourage their children to be unselfish, to think about the feelings of the other players, to give some thought to what is best for everybody. One technique a lot of coaches use is to employ plural pronouns rather than personal pronouns. Tell your children that it's not about "you," it's about "us." It's not about "me," it's about "we." And then walk your talk. Go to the team meetings. Get to know the other parents. Let your child hear you using the words "we" and "us." Get to know the other kids, too. Say hi to them. Compliment them. Cheer for them. Think about it: doesn't your child feel special when somebody else's mom or dad recognizes them or says something nice to them?

Of course they do. So be one of those parents who say something nice to the other kids. That will demonstrate to your own child that it's not just about "me," it's also about "us." And if the kids see all the parents cheering for all the teammates, they just might start cheering for each other.

One of the most negative elements of human nature is selfishness. Selfish people are not well liked. They usually become ostracized. When it's all about "me," a person isn't going to have very many friends. No parents want that for their children. So resolve now to help your kids overcome their natural desire to be self-centered. Be adamant about having a caring attitude. Insist on respect toward teammates. And convey to them *why* these things are important.

Competition and Fun

Youth sports introduce younger kids to athletic competition, often for the first time in their lives. They discover how to set small goals to get to their "want to"—and how to excel at one or more athletic skills. They experience winning and losing—and learn how to deal with their feelings regarding both.

As individuals, children react differently to competition. Some get very upset at a loss, others take it in stride. Some love to win games and some couldn't care less. Parents often set the stage for their children's reactions and responses to winning or losing. Depending on how they approach sports competition, the impact on their children can either be healthy or unhealthy.

Many parents feel it's necessary for their children to have a "winning attitude" when it comes to sports. But some translate that literally—meaning that their kids have to win ball games. They think that if the kids don't win those games, then they are failing. Such an attitude, however, is misguided.

Most teams do not win every game. Does that mean the kids are failures every time the team loses? Of course not. The last thing any parent should want their child to believe is that they are a failure. It's simply not healthy. It can cause the child to withdraw, to rebel, and to pull away from parents. It can lead to low self-esteem and, if the pressure to win is taken too far, it can do some serious psychological damage—damage that can last well into adulthood.

Parents should never, ever emphasize the score—either during or after a game. The younger kids don't pay much attention to the score anyway. They are wrapped up in participating in the game, in being with their friends, and in having a good time.

Surveys taken for decades in youth sports have shown at least one thing to be consistent: more than nine out of ten kids are just there for the fun of it.

Too much pressure on a child to win can not only do psychological damage, it can also take all the fun out of playing the game. Moreover, recent studies indicate not only that too much pressure harms a young athlete's performance on the field of play, and that having fun actually *enhances* a kid's performance. Peak performance is frequently achieved when athletes are enjoying themselves. It might have taken a sports "scientist" with formal statistics to prove this theory. But every kid who ever played in an organized league already knows it to be true.

As a parent, you should know it, too. You should allow your children to have fun while they're playing ball. And then you should sit back, relax, and take pleasure in the fact that they are enjoying themselves.

Tips for Parents

9/Nurturing the Team Concept

- Being part of a team helps young people learn mutual respect, mutual responsibility, and good communication.

- When parents seize opportunities to nurture the team concept, they provide their kids with an edge in dealing with people and give them a head start in life.

- Search for people who can help your child learn more about a sport. Encourage your child to build a mentoring relationship with that person.

- Kids need other people to help them achieve their dreams.

- Remember that sometimes the friendships your children form in youth leagues last a lifetime.

- Team sports can be the perfect forum for teaching your children selflessness and consideration for others.

- Employ plural pronouns rather than personal pronouns. Use "us" rather than "you"; "we" as opposed to "me."

- Get to know the other kids on your child's team. Say hi to them. Compliment them. Cheer for them.

- Parents set the stage for how children react to winning and losing.

- Never, ever emphasize the score to your child—either during or after a game.

- Putting too much pressure on your child to win can not only do psychological damage, it can also take all the fun out of the game.

- More than nine out of ten kids state that their main reason for being involved in sports is "to have fun."

- Peak performance is frequently achieved when athletes are enjoying themselves.

Work on your child's emotional infrastructure.
Develop it, build it, nurture it. It may be the most
important and the most rewarding thing you ever do.

Chapter 10
Looking Long-Term

Suppose you're an architect designing a home. If you design it only for the short term, you won't be overly concerned about the foundation lasting or the strengths of the walls or the beams in the ceiling. You'll be more concerned with appearances. You'll want it to look good, to be pleasing to the eye, to appeal to a buyer.

But if you're designing a home that will last, one that will still be standing strong eighty years from now, then you'll be focusing intently on the design of the infrastructure. You want the foundation to be solid and sturdy. You'll want the frame to have enough tensile strength so that the walls will not sag or the ceiling droop as time goes by. You might want the exterior walls to be made of brick rather than wood.

In a way, parents are like architects. Only they are not putting up homes, they're raising children. And like all great architects, the best parents are always looking long term. The values and lessons learned from sports are more important than the base hits, the goals scored, or the baskets made. The entire season means more than a single game. And a kid's overall childhood means more than a single season.

Values

There are many values that parents can instill in their children while utilizing youth sports as a vehicle. In fact, there are almost too many to name.

We've already discussed in some detail such things as teamwork and commitment. Another major principle frequently imparted to kids involved in sports involves personal responsibility. As a matter of fact, this value tends to be a common characteristic among the world's best athletes. They don't make excuses. They hold themselves personally accountable when they perform poorly.

When kids first start out in a team sport, they have a tendency to make up excuses when things don't go well. Some commonly heard excuses include the following:

"I struck out because the umpire called a ball a strike."

"I didn't get to play start at goalie because the coach doesn't like me."

"I missed that shot because something got in my eye."

"I didn't pass the ball to my teammate because she wasn't there in time."

Gradually, though, young athletes begin to understand that it's not the official's fault, or the coach's fault, or their teammate's fault, or anyone else's fault. They learn that they are accountable for their own actions.

Parents can and should make sure kids learn this valuable lesson. When your child comes home from a game and starts to make excuses, you should reinforce the principle.

"Don't blame it on the referee, Alex," you might say. "The referee didn't help the other team score six goals." Or "Don't blame it on your teammate, Lexi. She was wide open, you just didn't pass it to her." Or "Don't blame the coach because you didn't start. You have to work harder in practice and earn that starting spot."

Parents can help coaches teach their kids to take ownership of their own situations. Don't let them think of themselves as victims. Encourage them to look inward to see how they can become better athletes. Tell them that there's nobody to blame and that they should accept personal responsibility when things don't go their way. This is a lesson learned that will be valuable to your children far into their futures.

Another common characteristic of great athletes is the ability to overcome failure. The best hitters in baseball, for example, are successful only three or four times out of ten. That means they fail between sixty and seventy percent of the time.

Moreover, in virtually every sport, when a mistake is made, athletes have to put it behind them right away. Otherwise, the error will weigh on their minds. They will start to doubt themselves. And their coaches usually end up pulling them out of the game.

In life, as in athletics, if children give up every time they commit an error, then they'll never succeed in anything. Sports teaches kids to pick themselves up after they've fallen down. It teaches them to move on to the next play, or the next game. And if they lose the championship game, the mantra becomes "Just wait until next year."

Once again, parents can reinforce this principle at home and at the ball field. When your child makes an error, cheer them on from the sidelines. Call out to them, "Don't worry about it," or "It's okay," or "You'll get it the next time." And then remember not to dwell on your child's mistakes after the game. Accentuate the positive. Eliminate the negative.

Teach your children to view mistakes merely as stepping-stones to get to their goals. When they make an error on the field, they should forget about it and think about the next play. Teach your children to "shake it off."

As educated adults, you can probably think of many other values that can be gleaned from sports—values such as patience, flexibility, discipline, leadership, and fair play. And then there are all the elements of good character that your children can learn: hard work, caring, courage, honesty, and integrity. Just think of all the opportunities you have to teach your children meaningful principles that will last their entire lives.

Emotional Infrastructure

Most human behavior is a manifestation of security or insecurity, as the case may be. And whether or not a person is secure (and therefore effective) in life is anchored in three things:

1. **Self-esteem**
   Feeling that you can bring something to any effort
   Feeling esteemed as an individual

2. **Self-worth**
   Feeling that you have value as a human being
   Feeling pride in any endeavor of which your are a part

3. **Self-confidence**
   Feeling that you can do anything you set your mind to
   A byproduct of self-esteem and self-worth
   Self-esteem + Self-worth = Self-confidence

These three elements are the building blocks to personal effectiveness. They constitute the foundation of a person's emotional infrastructure—the way people feel about themselves.

In every person, self-esteem, self-worth, and self-confidence must be developed over an extended period of time. The most crucial time frame for such development is, of course, during childhood. And the people most able to effectively develop these elements in children are their parents.

That's you. It is your responsibility to make it happen. If you don't, the odds are greatly increased that when your children grow to adulthood, they will be insecure. That, in turn, can lead to all kinds of personal problems. On the other hand, if you do make it happen, then your children will be more likely to find a way to succeed in life on their own.

Sports can help kids feel good about themselves. It can provide a sense of purpose and worth that may not be available to children who are not involved in athletics. Belonging, for instance, is a major component of self-esteem. Therefore, just *being* on a team can help a kid garner some self-esteem.

Furthermore, the ability to overcome failure, or mistakes, is a major component of self-worth. People with low self-worth tend to be extremely cautious. They are often preoccupied with not making mistakes—usually because they have failed in the past and have not come back from those failures. Consequently, they actually see mistakes and failure as one and the same.

But if parents teach kids that mistakes are only stepping-stones to success, then the whole idea of "failure" is eliminated. An easy way to instill this lesson is to simply call attention to progress. Even the slightest bit of progress in attempting an athletic skill or mastering a new position can eliminate your child's fear of failure. And when fear is eliminated, self-confidence begins to develop.

Far too many parents seem to have unrealistic expectations of their children when they're on the athletic field. And when the kids don't rise to those perceived expectations, they feel bad. They lose hope that they'll ever be successful. And then they usually give up. Your children should not believe that you, as their parents, expect the impossible. Rather, you should constantly praise them when they do something well. You should encourage them when they make mistakes. And you should cheer them up when they're feeling low.

Rudy Ruettiger's parents worked hard to instill confidence in their son when he was young. They did not emphasize winning ball games. They were positive rather than negative, and they treated mistakes as learning experiences. After Rudy became a father himself, he realized how successful his parents were in developing his own emotional infrastructure. And when he looked back on it, Rudy realized that, when he was a kid, he never even knew it was happening. He was simply having fun the entire time.

So work on your child's emotional infrastructure. Develop it, build it, nurture it. It may be the most important and the most rewarding thing you ever do.

Unconditional Love and Support

When your child comes to you with a dream to be a professional athlete, you know in your heart that he or she is not likely to become another Michael Jordan or Mia Hamm. Even so, you should still encourage the dream. You should still encourage your children to believe that they can do anything, go anywhere, and be anybody or anything they want to be. Doing so not only lays the groundwork for a positive outlook on life, it also provides your kids with hope. And as we all know, hopes and dreams are the starting points for all human achievement.

We also know that many people lose hope and give up on their dreams too quickly. Others keep going. These are the people who are the achievers in life, the doers, the leaders. But what is it that keeps them going, that makes them persevere in the face of adversity? Some psychologists believe it has to do with a tremendous internal sense of security and self-confidence that is developed during childhood. They further believe that it is the unconditional love and support provided by mothers and fathers that nourishes the growth of both internal security and self-confidence.

Studies have shown that adult achievers were supported by their parents in whatever they tried. Their parents told them, "If you fail, we will still love you—no matter what."

As parents of Little Leaguers, you should do the same thing. Tell your children that if they try and fail, you will still love them—no matter what. Then take it a step further by demonstrating your unconditional love and support in a way that your children will believe you.

And how do you do that?

Be there for them. Show up to their games. Talk to them. Be a sounding board. Be patient and understanding. Provide them with advice and counsel in a manner that is positive, encouraging, and uplifting. Hug them often and tell them you love them often—especially during the times when they fail or are doubting themselves.

If you provide your children with unconditional love and support, they will not only learn a great deal from their experience in youth athletics, they'll enjoy it more. And that, in turn, will provide them with a strong foundation upon which they can grow and become well-adjusted, productive, and happy adults.

Tips for Parents
10/Looking Long-Term

- The season means more than a single game. And a kid's overall childhood means more than a single season.
- When your child comes home from a game and starts to make excuses, reinforce the principle of personal responsibility.
- When your kids make mistakes on the field, cheer them on from the stands. Accentuate the positive. Eliminate the negative.
- Teach your children to view mistakes merely as stepping-stones to get to their goals. Teach them to "shake it off."
- A person's internal security is anchored in three things:
  1. Self-esteem
  2. Self-worth
  3. Self-confidence
- Remember that the most crucial time for the development of a person's emotional infrastructure is childhood.
- Just being on a team can help a kid garner some self-esteem.
- Call your child's attention to even the slightest bit of progress.
- Don't forget that hopes and dreams are the starting points for all human achievement.
- Unconditional love and support provided by parents nourishes the growth of both internal security and self-confidence.
- Tell your children that you will love them "no matter what," and then make sure they really believe it.

Part III

Coaches

Because leadership is all about truth and character,
you should stay rooted in the belief that what you do on the field
of play, whether in practice or in a game, is exceedingly important.

Chapter 11
Preparing Yourself

Why are you involved in coaching? What is your motivation? Are you coaching to help kids in general? Are you coaching just to be sure your kid gets playing time? Is it pure community service? Is it because you love the sport and love working with kids? Is it all of these things? Spend some time thinking about it. It will drive a lot of what you do and it will show up in your relations with the kids.

Once you know *why* you're coaching, you then need to link it with the primary responsibility of every youth coach—to lead and mentor young athletes. These two key principles form a common thread through everything you will do as a coach.

Know the Sport You're Coaching

One of the most important things you can do as a coach is make sure you're working from a strong foundation of knowledge about your sport. You simply must be familiar with rules and fundamentals. Why? Because it will give you credibility with the kids. Don't forget that the kids are there to learn and that you, as the coach, are the person responsible for teaching and training them. You simply cannot go out there and wing it.

Understanding the sport you're coaching will give you confidence and decrease any frustration or anxiety you might have. The less frustrated you are and the more confident you become, the more effective you will be. It's almost a one-to-one ratio.

So get out there and equip yourself with as much knowledge as possible. You don't have to be an expert in the sport. You just have to get a handle on the basics. And there are plenty of ways to learn. Take a seminar. Read a book, get on the Internet, go to games, or watch some on television. Talk to people who are knowledgeable. As a matter of fact, it's a good idea to surround yourself with people who know the sport. So get out there and search for them. Maybe the parents of a kid on your team know the sport but, for whatever reason, cannot spend the time required to be a head coach. Ask them to show up to a practice every now and then. Inspire them to get involved. You can and should learn from them.

As a coach, if you do not have some knowledge of the sport you're coaching, it will be tough to connect with the kids. And *connecting with the kids* is what coaching is all about.

Resolve to Exemplify Integrity and Personal Excellence

In preparing yourself to be a coach, you should give serious consideration to how you are going to conduct yourself when interacting with the kids you'll be leading. Because leadership is all about truth and character, you should stay rooted in the belief that what you do on the field of play, whether in practice or in a game, is exceedingly important. With that in mind, you should resolve to exemplify integrity and hold yourself to the highest standard of personal excellence.

You should, for instance, treat everyone with respect and dignity. This includes umpires, opposing coaches and players and, most importantly, the kids on your own team. How *you* behave will directly affect how *they* behave. If you berate an umpire, so will they. If you don't shake hands with the opposing coach, they won't shake hands with the opposing players. You can't ask them to respect players and officials if you're not going to do so. And keep this in mind: once a coach starts to berate or make fun of *anybody*, things can go south very quickly. Don't let that snowball get started. Keep your personal standards high. And don't slip up—not even once.

Kids want to know their coach will always shoot straight with them, to know their coach will tell the truth. If you consistently maintain honesty and integrity, you'll more quickly earn trust and respect. You'll also be able to more effectively forge team unity and pride. Remember, kids will do anything for a coach if they know that the coach has their best interests at heart.

Exhibit a Positive Attitude

Developmentally, the years that children are involved in youth sports are extraordinarily important. A lot of coaches simply don't understand this fact. Don't be one of them.

Don't be one of the coaches who create an intense, competitive, "win at all costs" mentality on a team. That, in and of itself, keeps kids from reaching their peak potential. As a matter of fact, it can cause kids to go into a downward spiral. Pessimism from a coach can be a cancer that rapidly spreads through a team. Kids start to think, "I can't do this." They become lethargic, hesitant, and withdrawn. They retreat into a comfort zone that allows them to save face. And worst of all, they give up.

Understand that creating a positive environment is a key building block to self-worth, self-esteem and, therefore, self-confidence. It is the coach who creates such an environment. Resolve, then, to allow the kids on your team to take chances, to make mistakes and learn from them. Encourage your players to get back up after being knocked down.

It is developmentally critical that kids feel safe enough to make mistakes. Rather than being negative, the best coaches are upbeat and positive. They look ahead to future improvement. They tell kids that all things are possible if they work hard enough. They draw a link between "winning" and "learning from mistakes." And they maintain a "can-do" attitude that, ultimately, motivates and inspires players to rise to their peak potential.

The most talented and successful coaches find a way to touch the hearts of the kids on their teams. Exhibiting and maintaining a positive attitude is one of the keys to touching a kid's heart.

Key Coaching Principles
11/Preparing Yourself

- Ask yourself why you are involved in coaching.
- The primary responsibility of every youth coach is to lead and mentor young athletes.
- Equip yourself with as much knowledge as possible about the sport you're coaching. Get a handle on the rules and fundamentals.
- Surround yourself with people who know the sport.
- Stay rooted in the belief that what you do on the field of play is exceedingly important.
- Resolve to exemplify integrity and to hold yourself to the highest standard of personal excellence.
- Remember, how you behave will directly affect how your kids behave.
- Always shoot straight with the kids. Doing so will more quickly earn trust and respect—and more effectively forge team unity and pride.
- A positive environment for children is a key building block to self-worth, self-esteem and, therefore, self-confidence.
- Create an environment where it's safe for the kids on your team to go out and take chances.
- The best coaches are upbeat and positive.
- A "can-do" attitude motivates and inspires players.
- Remember, exhibiting and maintaining a positive attitude is one of the keys to touching a kid's heart.

Make sure that everybody understands the
agenda for the upcoming season. Involve the kids
in helping to create that agenda. And then get going.

Chapter 12
Setting Direction

The worst thing you can do when you first meet with the kids on your team is to start barking out orders at them. The best thing you can do is introduce yourself and begin talking about the future of the team.

Setting direction is all about creating clarity for the kids. It's about creating a common agenda, communicating expectations, setting standards, and ensuring that all players start the season on a level playing field. Communicating these things clearly is critical for a coach. At no time during the season do you want a player to come up to you and say, "I didn't know that," or "I didn't know we were expected to do this," or "I was unaware."

Create a Common Agenda

During one of your first practice sessions, have all the kids sit down in a circle and ask them some basic questions. "What are we going to do over the upcoming season? What do you want to accomplish? Why are we here?"

You might be surprised at some of the responses. They're not all going to say, "We want to win the league championship." Depending on their ages, they might say they want to win games, or have fun, or learn and improve their skills, or try a new position. Listen to them. If they're too quiet, ask some more specific questions. Do they want to be part of a team? Actually, all that most kids want is to be with their friends and play the game.

You should also let them know why *you* are there—and what you have to accomplish during the upcoming season. Tell them why you signed up to be their coach. Tell them that it's not all about winning games, that it's about learning life skills. Tell them that you want them to have fun, that you're going to help them improve their skills, and that you're going to teach them new positions, if that's what they want.

Some kids react negatively after initial preseason practices. Some say, "I don't want to do it." Others say, "I'm here because my dad wants me to be here," or "I really didn't want to do this, but my friend talked me into it." Your goal should be to keep *all* the kids in the fold. To that end, remember that kids are going to stick around if they believe they're going to get something out of it.

Once you create the connection between what they want and what you can provide them—you will win their hearts. Very few coaches do this well. But the best ones are great at it. Remember that one of the great football coach, Vince Lombardi's most famous sayings was, "First win the hearts of the people you lead, and they'll follow you anywhere."

Make sure that everybody understands the agenda for the upcoming season. Involve the kids in helping to create that agenda. And then get going.

Set Challenging Performance Standards

In one of the first practices, you should convey certain expectations to the players. Communicate the rules of engagement to them and lay a foundation for excellence. "I want a team committed to excellence," you might say. "Not a team that's content with being mediocre, or average, or just okay—but a team that wants to be *excellent.*"

Then make it clear that high performance standards are expected of *everyone*—not just those who think they're going to start. Everybody will have to hustle on and off the field; everybody will have to take their positions with class, dress with pride, and be held to high standards.

One baseball coach we know believes that the look of his team is very, very important. He wants his players to have the look of leaders—always hustling, everybody dressed the same way, everybody looking crisp and neat. For practices, each player must wear baseball pants, shoes, socks, a T-shirt, and a hat. During games, they all have to wear their uniforms the same way. Pinstripes on the shirt lined up with pinstripes on the pants. Black spikes with black laces. Pants pulled down to their calf muscles. Hats worn straight—no hair showing on their foreheads. And so on.

He also puts in place consequences if a player doesn't adhere to the standards. If you're not dressed correctly—you take a lap. If you don't hustle—you take a lap. Depending on the seriousness of the infractions, consequences go all the way up to being benched for the next game. But the coach is careful not to push a player into a downward spiral. So he gives a lot of positive feedback as well. "You look good today, Johnny." "Way to hustle, Kevin." "That's the way to take your position, Bobby!"

Why is it important to set challenging performance standards? Why should you have the kids hustle? Why should you want them to have the look of leaders?

Well, by clearly defining a set of guidelines that all players must abide by, a coach places everybody on a level playing field—star athletes, average athletes, and poor athletes. Insecure players get a sense of hope and self-worth. "Gosh, these other guys have to work as hard as I do," they think. "We also have to dress the same. Everybody has to take a lap if we screw up." As a result, they are more inspired to learn. They begin to grow, become more self-confident, and start to feel good about themselves.

The same is true for more confident players—who also learn a little humility and the important lesson that *every* member of the team has value. All the kids learn mental preparation, discipline, attitude, passion, and pride. These things can stay with them for the rest of their lives. An adult who learned those lessons as a kid might, for instance, make it a point to dress well when going to work.

When a coach first sets challenging performance standards, some kids may gripe about the new standards. That's natural. But after a while, something starts to tap their emotions and affect their senses. The *sight* of teammates running to their positions pumps them up mentally. The *touch* of their uniforms makes them feel good. When they *hear* their buddies talking each other up, they become encouraged. And eventually, they can *taste* it. They can *taste* victory. They can sense something unusual and special is happening. And then they feel like winners.

In the long run, challenging performance standards pull the kids together in a common bond. They also elevate the entire team with respect to mental attitude, optimism, and, ultimately, performance.

Emphasize Teamwork

Once you've created a common agenda and laid a foundation for excellence, you can start to communicate one of the most important lessons your players will ever learn—how to be part of a team. Kids are not naturally inclined to work together. They think about themselves first and others second. From the time they enroll in school, they are programmed to strive for individual achievement. As a coach, you have to overcome both the programming and the natural tendency to do things alone. After all, you're coaching a *team*. It's your job to take a group of young individuals and get them to function together as a cohesive unit.

Good coaches send out consistent messages about "team." They say things like, "Team is more important than any one individual." "It's not just a few players working hard or a few players working together—it's everybody working hard and working together." "You can get more done with a team than you can as an individual." "You are limited as an individual, but as part of a team, anything is possible."

Kids won't really believe these statements until they see the results for themselves. So you have to make certain that you do not allow one player to do it all—especially if that player happens to be your own child. Sometimes, it can be tough if the coach's kid is the best player on the team. Blood is thicker than water; there's no doubt about it. But even though Pat is the best athlete on the team, the team can't win if Pat is the only player on the field. As a coach, you simply cannot allow your kid—or any kid—to do it all. It flies in the face of teamwork.

Most kids think that if they're not playing, they're not contributing. Some coaches think that way, too. But in a true team, *everybody* can contribute. *Everybody* has value. Youth athletics is the perfect place to learn these lessons. And a coach is the perfect person to teach them.

Make certain that everybody on your team realizes they have an important role. Take time to speak with each player individually about the importance of his or her job, about how that player contributes to the team.

"Defense is just as important as offense—and let me tell you why." "Outfielders are just as important as pitchers—and let me tell you why." "You're the sixth starter on the basketball team. That's an incredibly important role—and let me tell you why."

For a lot of kids, just knowing their roles are important will help them feel a part of the team. It will make them feel included—that they're part something bigger than themselves. When players elevate themselves in importance, the effect is to elevate the entire team. That, in turn, also raises the group norm and leads to better team performance.

Make sure all your players understand that there's a greater good—and it's called "TEAM." Teach them that wins and losses are not to be associated with any one individual—but with everybody. Remember what Mike Krzyzewski (Coach K) says: "We win and we lose together."

Key Coaching Principles

12/Setting Direction

- When you first start meeting with the kids, introduce yourself and begin talking about the future direction of the team.

- Create a common agenda. Ask the kids why they are there and what they want to get out of the experience. Also let them know why *you* are there and what *you* want to accomplish.

- Remember, kids are going to stick around if they believe they're going to get something out of it.

- Don't forget what Vince Lombardi said: "First win the hearts of the people you lead and they'll follow you anywhere."

- Communicate the rules of engagement and lay a foundation for excellence.

- Make it clear that high standards are expected of everyone.

- Put in place consequences if a player does not adhere to the standards—and give a lot of positive feedback for the kids who do.

- Remember that kids are not naturally inclined to work together with others. They think about themselves first.

- It's your job to get all the players to function together as a cohesive unit.

- Send out consistent messages revolving around "team."

- Do not allow one player to do it all.

- Teach the kids that, in a true team, everybody can contribute and everybody has value.

- Take time to speak with each player individually about his or her role on the team.

The best coaches treat each player separately and uniquely.
The only way to do that effectively is to build a personal relationship
with every kid on your team.

Chapter 13
Connecting with the Kids

Think back about some people (a coach, a teacher, a parent) who had a profound impact on you when you were young. What did they do differently? And how did they do it?

Whatever it was, it really meant something to you, didn't it? However they did it, they really made you feel special and important, didn't they?

The truth is they connected with you. The best coaches do so naturally and with ease. Rather than just trying to win ball games, they believe that youth athletics are a vehicle to build emotional bonds with kids. They are able to bridge what is happening on the field with the personal aspirations of each and every player on their team. As a result, they not only win with the kids, they also win ball games.

Build a Relationship with Each Player

The players on your team are as different as the colors of the rainbow and as special as your own children. And they should be treated accordingly. Most novice coaches try to treat everybody exactly the same. But the best coaches treat each player separately and uniquely. They learn *who* their players are as individuals, *what* makes each different from the others, and *why* each one is special. The only way to do that effectively is to build a personal relationship with every kid on your team.

Sounds like a lot of work, doesn't it? Well, it is! But it doesn't have to be difficult work. As a matter of fact, once you get the hang of it, it can be a lot of fun. And you can rest assured that it will pay off in the long run.

When starting a relationship, a coach needs time, patience, and a little savvy about human nature. Rome wasn't built in a day—and neither is an effective relationship. So begin your relationship-building in the preseason. Be patient with the kids. Allow them to develop their friendships with you in *their* time, not yours. And here's an important tip on human nature: the kids will form initial opinions of you, and set behaviors toward you, based on your first few minutes of contact with them. If you make them feel uncomfortable or threatened, an emotional psychological barrier will go up. And if a kid builds that wall too high, you will not be able to get near them emotionally. They simply will not let you in. So the best thing to do is not let that wall go up in the first place.

Here are three key steps to creating a successful relationship:

Step #1: First Listen

It's a good idea to meet with each player in an environment that is comfortable to them—perhaps in their own home with their parents. Approach slowly, softly, and carefully. Don't push. Your goal is to find what it is within each player that really means something to them. So ask them. What is important to you? What position do you want to play? What is your dream?

Some kids may want to grow up to be professional athletes. Some may want to be a writer, a doctor, a plumber. Some may just want to get into college. Others may not be able to articulate any dreams or aspirations. With them, you may have to do a little detective work. But you must search for something to which that particular kid will respond—perhaps an idea that really means something to them.

Rudy Ruettiger's high-school football coach did something very simple, yet very important for Rudy. He listened to him. Rudy came up and said, "Coach, I want to play football for the University of Notre Dame. What do you think?" Many coaches might have responded by saying, "You're too small. It's not possible. Get another dream." But Coach Gordie Gillespie responded by saying, "You know what, Rudy? If anybody can do it, you can." And of course, five foot, seven inch Rudy Ruettiger went on to become the most famous player in the history of Notre Dame football.

Why did Rudy respond to that little bit of hope given to him by his coach? Because a more powerful person, an adult he admired, gave him encouragement. And every single kid, without exception, will respond to that kind of encouragement *if he knows his coach cares about him*. And that brings us to the second step in creating a successful relationship.

Step #2: Show You Care

Why should you show kids you care about them?

Because caring is a big motivator. Huge! In fact, it may be the single most important weapon in your motivation arsenal. Why? Because, psychologically, when coaches really care about their players, it puts the kids in a position of strength and receptivity to begin building self-worth, self-esteem, and self-confidence.

But words alone are not enough. As a coach, you have to *show* the kids you care. And you already have a head start in that area. The previous one-on-one time you spent listening is a big indicator to the kids that you care. Also, you're now armed with key information about each player. Now you know the buttons you can push to motivate them. Your next move is to tie what is happening on the field of play with each player's personal aspirations.

Here's one way to do it:

When you're challenging the players to get to practice on time, to dress the part, to hustle—remind them of their dreams. Then explain to them how these things specifically will help them achieve those dreams. For example, you might say, "Listen, Pat, you're never going to get into college if you don't learn to work hard, to dress well, and to show up to work on time." And then you might say, "That's why I need you to get to practice on time. That's why I need you to dress the part. That's why I want you to hustle." Often, the kids' responses and reactions will be amazingly positive.

Now you're connecting. Now you're creating a sense of comfort for your players. They know you're teaching them a life lesson that will help them achieve their dreams. They're thinking, "This is good. I'm okay here. I'm learning."

Your relationship has now progressed to the point where you can give hard-hitting feedback and the kids will not have the immediate reaction that you're attacking them personally. Now you're ready for the final step in your quest to build a quality relationship.

Step #3: Earn Trust

As a coach, you want your players to have confidence in you. You want them to rely on your honesty, your integrity, and your friendship. You want them to believe in you—to believe that what you tell them is the truth. In other words, you want them to trust you.

The fact is that every successful relationship is built on a strong foundation of trust. There are no exceptions. Kids, however, will not automatically grant you their trust. You have to earn it. As a matter of fact, every coach has to go through the first two steps in order to have a prayer of earning a kid's trust. After that, it's a matter of hard work and consistency over time. It means keeping your word, being fair, and applying the rules equally to everybody. It means walking your talk and never, ever lying to a player.

The kids on your team have to believe that your motives are pure. If they know that you're really there to help them, not just to use them as a means of winning games, you'll be able to motivate them to do just about anything. If they don't know that, they'll only go through the motions.

Vince Lombardi once said, "You can't hoodwink the players." He was right. The kids will know instantly if your motives aren't pure. Remember this: Once you've earned a player's trust, be sure you don't do anything to lose it. Why? Because lost trust is nearly impossible to regain.

On the other hand, lasting trust leads to lasting loyalty. When a kid knows you care and knows you'll always shoot straight—*that's* when a kid will say, "I'd go through a brick wall for my coach."

Assess Individual Skills and Knowledge

While you're working at building relationships with the players, you should also be assessing their skills and knowledge. In gauging the knowledge level of your team, you should be finding answers to questions like these: What are the kids' individual levels of understanding of the basics in your sport? How much detailed knowledge do they possess about the sport? Where do they stand physically, developmentally, and emotionally?

Regarding levels of skill and physical talent, you should be evaluating each player in regard to their basic abilities of dribbling, passing, spiking, running, batting, throwing, kicking, et cetera (whatever critical skills are needed to excel at the sport in which you're coaching). Once you've made your basic assessments about each player—and, of course, established personal relationships with them—it's time to have one-on-one conversations about strengths and weaknesses.

Rather than meeting in their homes, this time it would be better to pull the kids aside in practice—one at a time for about five minutes each. At this point, they're in the athletic arena and that means it's time to work. As you begin your conversation, smile, accentuate the positive, and avoid using negative words like "weaknesses."

"Okay, Terry," you might say, "I think you are really excellent at passing. That is clearly one of your strengths."

Then, remembering that every conversation is two-way, you might ask the youngster, "What do you think?"

After hearing what the kid has to say (and taking it into account), start talking about development. "I'd like to begin working on a few things that will help you get to your dream of playing at the professional level. One thing you could improve upon, I think, is dribbling and moving the ball faster toward the goal. Let's use these next few sessions as opportunities to practice and improve in those areas. Okay? As a matter of fact, if you're willing, I'll stay an extra fifteen minutes tomorrow to work with you one-on-one. What do you say?"

Most kids will respond by saying, "Sure, Coach, that'd be great." Then, when they get home, they'll tell their parents about the extra time their coach is going to give them after the next practice. And it will be something they'll look forward to with eagerness and anticipation.

As you have similar conversations with all the players, you should also be thinking about the team as a whole—its capabilities, its strengths, and its opportunities to improve. One of the reasons a coach assesses players individually is to determine what their roles will be on the team.

During the regular season, many novice youth coaches haphazardly rotate the players around to different positions. The best coaches, however, realize this is not a good idea. Kids need to be placed where their talents are best brought to bear. It's appropriate not only for the individual, but for the team as a whole. If a youngster is told to play shortstop when he's not able, he might be embarrassed. And a kid who knows how to play the position well, yet is placed in the outfield, might become frustrated.

One of the main responsibilities of a coach is the performance of the entire team. If Johnny wants to pitch, but he's not one of the better pitchers on the team, and he can play third base better than anybody else—he has to be placed at third base. A good coach will make certain that Johnny knows the reason *why* he's being asked to play third base—and then coached on the proper skills so that he can make the pitching staff.

In determining the role each kid will play, it's a good idea to ask the youngsters what they think. After most of the preseason practices have been completed, they'll know who the good players on the team are. And they'll have a pretty good idea of where they will fit in.

If, for instance, you've got two kids vying for the starting quarterback position, you might ask the two candidates for their opinions. One of the kids might surprise you and say, "Coach, I know that Roger is the best. He should start." If that happens, and you agree with the assessment, then your decision has just been made a whole lot easier.

Involving the players in the team-building process is a very smart thing to do. In addition, good coaches do not exclude any member of the team from having a meaningful role. Everybody must be involved in the team effort. And everybody must understand their role and be motivated to perform it with excellence. Even the twelfth player on the basketball team—who may not see much game time—will contribute willingly in practice if she knows she is helping the team by forcing the other players to perform to their peak potentials.

Great coaches value every member of the team—and they find a way for everyone to have an impact and contribute in a meaningful way.

Employ the "Heart, Head, and Hands" Framework

Take out a sheet of paper and list all the players on your team in a column on the left side. Across the top, write "Heart," "Head," and "Hands." Now you have a simple framework for assessing the dreams, knowledge, and skills of the kids on your team.

In the column titled "Heart," list the dreams, aspirations, and goals of each kid. Matt wants to play pro ball; David wants to go to college; and so on.

Under "Head," jot down notes about that kid's level of understanding of the sport. This is Katie's first year; she needs to learn the basics. Danny's in his fourth year; he's a captain on the court.

"Hands" refers to specific skill levels. Steve: terrific fielder; work on batting. Olivia: good at defense; focus on shooting. Jessica: great spiker; work on serves.

Most novice coaches go straight for the "Hands." Don't be one of them. Get to know the whole kid. Build a relationship. Assess knowledge and skills—Heart, Head, and Hands. Then you will be ready to take the entire team to a higher level.

Remember, if you go through an entire season and have connected with each kid, if you know what makes each and every player on your team tick, *then* you will have had a successful season.

Player Name	Heart	Head	Hands
Steve			
David			
Katie			
Jessica			
Danny			
Olivia			
Matt			

Key Coaching Principles

13/Connecting with the Kids

- Learn *who* your players are as individuals, *what* makes each different from the others, and *why* each one is special.

- When starting relationships, have patience with the kids. Allow them to develop their friendships with you in *their* time, not yours.

- Remember the three key steps to a successful relationship:

  1. First Listen

  2. Show You Care

  3. Earn Trust

- Caring may be the single most important weapon in your motivation arsenal.

- Tie what is happening on the field of play with each player's personal aspirations.

- Remember that every successful relationship is built on a foundation of trust. There are no exceptions.

- In gauging the knowledge level of your team, assess each player's understanding of the basics in your sport, what detailed knowledge they possess, and where they are physically, developmentally, and emotionally.

- Be sure to spend time one-on-one with each of the players on your team.

- Don't forget that one of the main responsibilities of a coach is the performance of the *entire* team.

- Ask the players what they think. Involve them in the team-building process.

- Value every member of the team. Find a way for everyone to have an impact and contribute in a meaningful way.

It is every coach's responsibility to create and maintain an atmosphere where players learn willingly and enthusiastically.

Chapter 14
Teaching and Developing

coach, n. a person who teaches or trains athletic teams; a private teacher. —v. "to teach; to prepare and develop."

This is what you'll read if you look up the word "coach" in the dictionary. And if you ask kids what they expect from their coach, you'll almost always hear something similar to, "I expect my coach to teach me the sport and make me a better player."

One of the most important things about being a coach is teaching higher-level athletic skills. From the very first practice, through the regular season to the last team meeting—the most effective coaches work to increase both the individual's and the team's knowledge, abilities, and talents. The best coaches also make certain that the players feel themselves improving as they go, so that by the end of the season, the players realize how much they've learned.

Create a Learning Environment

In the wrong environment, kids can stagnate. Too much pressure to perform, for instance, may cause them to hold back.

And too much comfort can result in a lack of motivation. Either way, the result is almost always underperformance.

But in the right environment, kids can blossom. With the proper level of discipline, they can be motivated to perform at high levels. And with the appropriate level of comfort, they will not be afraid to get up and try again after making a mistake.

It is every coach's responsibility to create and maintain an atmosphere where players learn willingly and enthusiastically—where the atmosphere has just the right balance of both discipline *and* comfort. As a coach, if you adhere to the following three points, you will be successful in creating an effective learning environment.

1. Provide Ongoing Feedback

Players should always know how their coaches think they're performing. This means providing both positive comments and constructive criticism. Kids need to be told when they are doing something well, so they'll keep doing it that way. They also need to know when they're not doing something well, so they can focus on improvement.

Basic group dynamics tells us that it's best to interact with a team by starting with the individuals who compose it. When providing feedback, for instance, you should take kids aside during practices. Speak softly to them. Give them some of your personal time. But remember that when you're one-on-one with players, never, ever yell at them. Doing so tends to take the kids down a notch. And a coach's job is to *raise* the players' level of self-confidence, not lower it.

When you provide ongoing feedback to the members of your team, you are doing what every coach must do to be successful: you are communicating with them. Just remember one of the cardinal rules of coaching: praise in public, criticize in private.

2. Focus on Behavior Rather than Attitude

Many youth coaches try to motivate players by focusing on attitudes. They might say, "You're not hustling because you don't care," or "You look lousy," or, the old standby, "You've got a bad attitude."

But the best coaches never say things like that to a player. Why? Because doing so usually causes the kid to do *less*, rather than more. Adults might be able to handle a coach who focuses on attitude, but kids usually cannot. Their young minds and emotions are simply too fragile.

If you want to create a learning environment, you must focus on behaviors rather than attitudes. Here are a few easy tips to remember:

First, set clear expectations. Say things like, "I expect you to show up to practice on time," or "I expect you to hustle and work hard at practice," or "I expect you to have your shirt tucked in both at practice and games."

Second, talk to the kids specifically about what they need to do to improve—and then focus on those particular things.

Third, hold the kids accountable for their actions. Institute some discipline. If a kid doesn't hustle, it's okay to have him take a lap. Just be consistent about how you dole out disciplinary actions. Remember to focus on the fact that the kid didn't hustle, rather than the kid's reason for not hustling.

You cannot change attitudes by hammering on players. But when you get them *behaving* in the proper manner, attitudes will begin to improve.

3. Encourage Players to Learn from Mistakes

If you ask kids what they like about their favorite coaches, the answer usually revolves around how mistakes were handled. Here are some common responses:

"He never makes me feel like I screwed up."

"She may correct me, and she may be passionate, but she never crosses the line and makes me feel stupid."

"He always asks me what we can learn from the mistake. Then I'll try again and, eventually, I'll get it right."

"She makes me feel good about myself—even when I'm not performing well."

Everybody makes mistakes, but not everybody learns from mistakes. As a coach, part of your job is to see that your players learn from their errors, rather than become dejected by them. If you provide positive feedback when players are down, you'll find that they will respond "positively."

And think about this: Your approach in handling mistakes can have a profound impact on how kids will deal with adversity—not only during the season, but for the rest of their lives. That is one of the great byproducts of creating a true learning environment. Rather than buckling when faced with adversity, kids will actually become more confident. Rather than becoming dejected with each defeat, they will garner new resolve—and become more inspired than ever.

Conduct Organized and Disciplined Practices

Most of the time you spend with the players on your team is during practice sessions. This is where you get to know them, where they get to know you, and where you teach them the finer points of the game. Practice is also where you take a group of individuals and turn them into a team.

If you're going to be a good coach, your practice sessions should be well organized, disciplined, and challenging. That sounds pretty basic, but you'd be amazed at how many youth coaches allow their practices to become a free-for-all. By just letting the kids wing it, all they get is a cluster bubble. And that does not lead to teamwork.

Psychologically, a well-structured and disciplined practice creates a level of comfort for kids. When they understand what's going to happen over the next two hours, and when they get used to the routine, apprehension is relieved, confidence begins to build, and they become more open-minded.

First-rate practices also create clarity. When the kids know *what* is expected of them, and *when* it is expected, they are less likely to goof off. As a matter of fact, with an element of anticipation, the kids usually become focused and energized.

Many effective youth coaches utilize the following six-step blueprint for practice sessions:

1. **The First Five Minutes**
   - Start on time
   - Pull all the kids together and ask them to "listen up"
   - Tell them the plan for the practice
     o Be as specific as possible
     o Make sure everyone knows what is expected
   - Ask the players if they have any questions

2. **Warm Up** (ten minutes)
   - Get the energy going physically
     o Stretching; calisthenics; jogging, et cetera.
   - Prime them mentally
     o Tell them you are going to challenge them
     o Tell them that sometime during practice, there will be a mental push that will test them physically
     o Ask them, "Will you be ready for the push?"

3. **Break Into Stations** (thirty to forty-five minutes)
   - Split the team into smaller groups
     - Offense, defense, infielders, outfielders, whatever makes sense
   - Set up a variety of drills and activities
     - Fundamentals (passing, dribbling, hitting, batting, etc.)
     - Higher level skills
   - Rotate at regular intervals
     - Call out, "Move on" (allows players to get used to the sound of your voice)

4. **Practice Game Situations** (thirty to forty-five minutes)
   - Keep the team in smaller groups
     - Offense, defense, infielders, outfielders, whatever makes sense
   - Teach the players to visualize various game situations.
     - "Bases loaded, two outs, single to right field, what do you do?"
     - Explain what they need to do, including where each player should be positioned, and explain why it works
   - Repeat until the players get it right
   - This is a good place to insert the "mental push" you challenged them with during the warm-up
   - Vary game situations in practice over the course of the season (based on need and timing)

5. **Scrimmage** (thirty to forty-five minutes)
   - Pull the entire team back together
   - Divide into teams

o Over the course of the preseason, put the starting team together and let them get used to playing with each other

· Conduct a full scrimmage so the players can get used to real game activity

· Stop the activity every now and then to explain mistakes or to praise excellence

· This is also a good place to insert the "mental push" you challenged them with during the warm-up

6. The Final Five Minutes

· Gather the kids around

· Give them feedback

o Ask them how *they* thought they did

o Tell them how *you* thought they did

o Address both physical and mental aspects

· Explain what comes next

o "Practice tomorrow. We'll work on these things."

o "Game on Saturday at 9 AM. Here's the plan."

· End the practice on time

Use practice time to cultivate and build relationships (with and among the kids) and to develop critical skills and talents. Remember that practices should be dynamic and ever-changing. As skill levels increase, they should be taken to a higher level. What was appropriate early in the season may be inappropriate later in the season.

Practice sessions are principally about preparation for games. If the kids look forward to them with excitement and anticipation—then you'll find that exceptional performance during games will usually be the result.

Teach Life's Lessons

On the surface, coaching is all about teaching players about the sport. But below the surface lies a much broader, more important, and deeper meaning. Coaching is really about the kids. The sport is secondary. The sport is the vehicle a coach uses to connect with each kid, to mold character, and to teach life's lessons.

A disciplined and well-organized practice, for example, is really more about teaching a youngster to be on time, to be focused, and to respect and work well with other members of their team. Providing ongoing feedback is really more about learning from mistakes and setbacks. It's about teaching kids that everybody makes mistakes and that, after making an error, they need to pick themselves up and get back in the game. Focusing on behavior rather than attitude helps kids learn how to handle defeat. There will be times in life when they are victorious and there will be times when they'll be defeated. Coaches teach kids how to be humble in victory and proud in defeat.

After you build strong enough relationships with the kids on your team, you then have the opportunity to expand your influence with them beyond the athletic field: how they interact with their siblings and friends, how they treat their parents, proper study habits and the importance of making good grades in school. A coach can talk with kids about all these things and more.

Every psychologist in the world will confirm that, as a coach, you can have a profound effect on the youngsters on your team. The truth is, though, that whether you like it or not, you *will* have *some* impact. The question is whether or not your impact will be positive or negative.

When asked who had influenced them when they were kids, adults will often mention a teacher or a coach. They'll cite something that happened during a season where their coach may have taken the event and applied it to a life lesson, or told a story that touched them, or created real meaning from a seemingly simple situation.

Many coaches create relationships that go far beyond the athletic arena. They forge relationships that last a lifetime for both themselves and the kids. In turn, that creates a deeper meaning for people who would call themselves "coach."

One person we spoke with told us he had been coaching for a long time and, with time, had forgotten why he began coaching in the first place. "I got consumed by all the wrong things," he said. "I got all wrapped up in winning games and beating the other coaches. For a while, it was all about me—not the kids. But I finally got back to the true meaning of being a coach. It's about being a teacher and friend to all these youngsters. I started out coaching my own kids. They're all grown up now, but I'm still a coach. I'll guess I'll always be a coach."

Key Coaching Principles
14/Teaching and Developing

- One of the most important things about being a coach is teaching higher-level athletic skills.
- Adhere to the following three principles in creating an effective learning environment:
  1. Provide Ongoing Feedback
  2. Focus on Behavior, Rather than Attitude
  3. Encourage Players to Learn from Mistakes
- Remember one of the cardinal rules of coaching: Praise in public, criticize in private.
- When a coach gets players behaving in the proper manner, attitudes will begin to improve.
- A well-structured and disciplined practice creates both clarity and a level of comfort for kids.
- Utilize the following six-step blueprint for practice sessions:
  1. The First Five Minutes
  2. Warm Up
  3. Break Into Stations
  4. Practice Game Situations
  5. Scrimmage
  6. The Final Five Minutes
- Remember that practices should be dynamic and ever-changing. As skill levels increase, they should be taken to a higher level.
- Practice sessions are principally about preparation for games.
- Remember that coaching is really about the kids. The sport is secondary.
- Teach life's lessons.

Game day is a time to be serious yet lighthearted,
intense yet calm, determined yet patient. It is also a time
for you, as the head coach, to set a good example for your players.

Chapter 15
Focusing on Game Day

All coaches use practice sessions to prepare for games. But the really great coaches understand that the whole point of the athletic endeavor is to perform on game day.

It is in games where the players show what they've learned, where they demonstrate their improved skills, and where they reveal their hearts and character. It is also in games where you, as a coach, bring everything to bear—your knowledge of the sport; your relationships with the kids; your assessment of their head, heart, and hands; and your own personal excellence. Everything comes together on game day.

Remember that the season is a long one—with many games and many opportunities to learn and grow. You should treat each game separately, yet consistently and with the same process.

Develop a Game Plan

People who describe their most effective coaches consistently mention the fact that these coaches provide a strategy

117

that revolves around how their team will beat the competition. They study in detail the strengths and weaknesses of each upcoming opponent. They think about how the strengths of their own team can be employed to gain an advantage. Then they develop a strategic, well-thought-through game plan that is quickly presented to the players. And that plan is often rehearsed in pregame practice sessions—sometimes over and over again until the players get it right.

An effective game plan is always linked to the strengths and capabilities of individual team members. "Okay, kids," the coach might say, "Our next opponent has a really strong offensive player who scores a lot if allowed to go uncontested. Since J.J. is our best defensive player, I want J.J. to cover this kid." Or another coach might say, "This team uses a zone defense almost all the time—so we're going to go with our outside three-point shooters. We've got to feed the ball to Chris and Terry and encourage them to shoot more."

The best coaches will also ensure that *all* players are aware of *all* the details of the game plan. Some kids may not be the strategic focus during this game, but they probably will be at some point during the season. Substitute players must be able to slip into the game on a moment's notice in the event of any unforeseen circumstances, such as an injury or foul trouble. If all players know the details of the game plan, they feel included as part of the team and will therefore more likely provide encouragement to their teammates from the bench or the field.

There are three very practical reasons for linking your game strategy to the abilities of the players on your team.

First, it trains the kids to focus—to keep their minds on the game. When they're engaged in all aspects of the strategy, there is less dillydallying on the bench. They tend to stay focused and more motivated during the game and, ultimately, over the course of the season.

Second, it educates the kids on all aspects of the sport and helps them learn to anticipate. In basketball, for instance, non-starters learn to count team and individual fouls and prepare to substitute on a moment's notice. In baseball, if the starting pitcher is throwing too many pitches, the reserve pitchers know it's time to start warming up.

Third, it helps the team win ball games. Your team is composed of your players. When you focus strategically on utilizing all the strengths and talents of your team, you will more often come up victorious.

In addition to these very practical reasons for linking your game plan directly to the individual players, there are also a number of psychological and motivational grounds. For one thing, it helps instill clarity for the kids. As the players begin to connect the dots and understand what they're preparing for, they increasingly become mentally prepared for the game. And don't forget that mental preparation is every bit as important as physical preparation—perhaps even more so.

Furthermore, by involving the kids directly in the game plan, you make it personally relevant to them. Psychologically, this is a vital point. Why? Because when kids believe that something is not important, interesting, or personally relevant to them—they will check out mentally. In these cases, their minds wander, they goof off, or they simply give you that deer-in-the-headlights stare.

At the end of the day, kids are human beings. They want to feel good about themselves. And when they're included, they just naturally feel good. They also tend to feel more secure in their environment. And don't forget that most behavior is a manifestation of security or insecurity. So anytime you as a coach can help your players feel more secure, you'll begin to see confidence grow. Confidence then leads to a more positive attitude and a belief that success can be achieved.

Stay Focused and Keep the Players Attentive

Game day is the time to implement the plan you've developed. It's a time to be serious yet lighthearted, intense yet calm, determined yet patient. It is also a time for you, as the head coach, to set a good example for your players.

Don't forget that you have resolved to exemplify integrity and personal excellence. To do so, you should prepare yourself mentally before the game. Review the game plan. Be well rested. Don't bring your personal problems to the field of play. Your players deserve your entire focus and commitment. They have earned your respect, so give them your best effort.

When you're out there, remember to treat everyone with respect and dignity—the referees, the opposing players and coaches, *and* the members of your own team. You are not going to yell at your players if they make a mistake. You are going to take them aside privately for a quick word of encouragement. "That's okay, Chris," you'll say. "This is what you did wrong. We'll work on it in practice. Shake it off. Everybody makes an error now and then. Get 'em next time."

Like it or not, you are a role model for these young people. Your players will emulate you because you are their coach. Resolve to be a positive influence, rather than a negative one.

Once you have prepared yourself to behave with integrity and personal excellence, you will be ready to coach the players during the game. In order to be effective, you simply must maintain open channels of communication with everybody on the team—whether they are in the field or on the bench.

Accordingly, you must have every player's eyes and ears. All the kids should be taught to respond to your voice during the game—and, during breaks in the action, to look you straight in the eye when you're talking to them. A key rule for your team should be, "When the coach speaks, everybody pays attention—no exceptions."

In addition, you should encourage the players to talk to you. Listen to them. Hear what they have to say. And also encourage them to talk to each other. Let them adjust on their own when necessary. But keep them on the right path when they start to deviate.

While the game is in progress, the very best coaches strategically link the game plan to what is actually happening on the field. They are always talking to the players—constantly reminding them about what they worked on in practice and how the game strategy is playing out. "Hey, kids," they'll say, "Remember when we worked on this situation in practice? Well, here it is. You all know what you're supposed to do. Here it is! We're ready! Let's go!"

Sometimes youth coaches get a little too wrapped up in the game and forget why they're out there in the first place and, more importantly, why the kids are out there in the first place. Be prepared for that ahead of time. Ask an assistant coach to say something to you if you seem to be losing perspective. Then correct your behavior.

Resolve always to be positive and encouraging toward the kids. And, for goodness' sake, don't put so much stress on them that they don't enjoy what they're doing. Don't forget to let the kids have fun.

Praise and Teach

After the game is over, a coach's job is not finished. It's only just begun.

How the team handles wins and losses, for instance, may influence their behavior for years to come. If they win, will they rub it in the face of the opposition? If they lose, will they become so dejected that they never pick themselves back up and try again? As a youth coach, it's up to you to set them straight from the beginning.

How the team acts when they win or lose should be consistent. Teach the kids to be humble in victory and upright in defeat. In victory, there is elation. Don't squelch that. Let the kids celebrate their victory. But teach them not to celebrate so much that they rub it in the faces of the players who just lost. Those kids are already feeling bad enough.

Rather, teach the kids to think about how the other team might be feeling at that moment—and remind them that *all the players* were trying to do the best they could. The proper behavior, therefore, is to be civil, to be decent, and to act like a good sport. Require your kids to shake hands with the other team after every game—whether they win or lose. Coach them to congratulate the other team on their effort and say, "Good game."

After you leave the field, but before everybody goes home, pull the kids together for a few minutes. Congratulate them for their efforts. Praise the team as a whole and acknowledge the individual standouts of the game. Recognize as many of the kids as possible, but don't mention everybody. Remember, if you recognize everybody, you end up recognizing nobody.

If the kids won their game, acknowledge the victory. "Okay, team, we won this game. Now let's highlight some things we did particularly well."

Then drive those things home: "We practiced well. We executed our game plan. This is how we won. This is why we won." Then reinforce the value of preparation. That will get the kids even more motivated for the next practice. They'll also begin to understand the value of planning, preparing, and practicing. Moreover, now's the time to start driving home some life lessons.

"We understood our competitor's strengths and weaknesses. We used our own strengths and strategically applied them to our game plan. We practiced that plan. We worked together as a team—not as a group of lone individuals, but as a *real* team. Our skills improved and, as a result, we gained confidence. All these things led to our victory. I want you all to remember that. These same things will help you be successful beyond sports— in whatever you do in the future."

If the kids lost their game, go easy on them. They are vulnerable to negative criticism and may be feeling a bit down. Often they'll have a tendency to blame others for their loss. But don't let them play the blame game. Sometimes you lose and there's no one to blame. Rather, encourage them to look at the things they did well. Praise them for their efforts. But also tell them that there were some things they could have done better. Tell them not to worry about it for now, that "we'll work on it in the next practice."

After a couple of days, the kids' negative emotions will be dissipated. That's when you want to analyze the defeat in some detail. Remember that players are more attentive after a loss than they are after a win. So there's a great opportunity for you to teach them something meaningful.

Sometimes, you just have to say to the team, "Hey kids, we blew it out there the other day. And let me tell you why we blew it." It's okay to say that. But then you must follow through on the reasons. First ask the players what they could have done better. They've had a couple of days to think about it and you might be surprised at how much they realize what went wrong. List all the things that need to be improved upon and then start working on those things in practice. If the kids know specifically what they need to do better, it is amazing how hard they will work to improve their skills.

Use a loss as an opportunity to drive home some more life lessons: "You have to find a way to pick yourself up," a coach should say to the players. "Channel your emotions. Think about what you could have done better. Put a corrective action plan in place. Practice that plan. And then go get 'em in the next game."

When you take every opportunity to praise and teach, you will be equipping your kids with skills they may use later as adults. And *that* is really what being a coach is all about.

Key Coaching Principles

15/Focusing on Game Day

- Treat each game separately, consistently, and with the same process.
- Develop a strategy that revolves around how your team is going to beat the competition. Link it to the strengths and capabilities of your players.
- Present your game plan to the players and rehearse it in practice.
- Once they feel secure and confident, the players will work more effectively in a team environment and their skills will dramatically improve.
- As a coach, you should prepare *yourself* mentally before each game.
- Resolve personally to exemplify integrity and personal excellence.
- Maintain channels of communication with everybody. Have all the players' eyes and ears.
- Talk to the players during the game. Strategically link the game plan to what is currently happening on the field of play.
- Teach the kids to be humble in victory and upright in defeat.
- Win or lose, require your players to shake hands with the other team after every game.
- After the game, pull the team together for a few minutes. If the game was a win, congratulate the players and reinforce the things that helped them win. If the game was a loss, go easy on the players. Never play the blame game.
- Analyze defeat in practice and teach life lessons.
- Don't forget to let the kids have fun.

About the Authors

Donald T. Phillips is a best-selling author of fourteen books. His trilogy on American leadership (*The Founding Fathers On Leadership, Lincoln On Leadership, Martin Luther King, Jr. On Leadership*) has won worldwide acclaim. *Lincoln On Leadership* paved the way toward the creation of an entire new genre of books on historical leadership. He has written two books with Duke basketball coach Mike Krzyzewski (Coach K) and one on the leadership style of legendary football coach Vince Lombardi. Mr. Phillips is also a well-known speaker and consultant. He has served three terms as mayor of his local town and has coached youth baseball and softball. He is the father of two sons and a daughter.

*   *   *

"NEVER GIVE UP ON YOUR DREAMS"

Known to millions as "the little guy with the big dream," **Daniel "Rudy" Ruettiger** is one of the most inspirational football players in the history of the University of Notre Dame. A living sports legend, he was immortalized in TriStar Pictures' blockbuster movie, *Rudy*, and is the spokesperson for a revolutionary line of sports drinks that bears his name. A highly sought-after motivational speaker, Rudy entertains and motivates school children, university students, professional athletes, and corporate audiences worldwide. He has shared speaking platforms with President George Bush, President Bill Clinton, Peter Lowe, Joe Montana, Colin Powell, Christopher Reeve, and many others.

Rudy is the founder of the Rudy Ruettiger Foundation, which develops and supports programs to help children build self-esteem, reach their full potential, and become positive role models. The foundation also sponsors the Rudy Award program for children who overcome obstacles and exemplify the qualities of character, courage, contribution, and commitment.

Rudy continues to influence and inspire athletes of all ages through The Rudy Movement (www.therudymovement.com).

*   *   *

Peter M. Leddy, PhD, is an organizational psychologist and sports psychology consultant, focusing on leadership in athletic coaching. Dr. Leddy is a member of the Exercise and Sports Psychology division of the American Psychological Association and the Association for the Advancement of Applied Sports Psychology. He also serves on the board of directors of the Rudy Ruettiger Foundation.

Dr. Leddy has designed and implemented successful leadership development programs for executives and managers in various Fortune 500 companies and has enjoyed more than twenty years of experience as a business executive with major corporations, including Invitrogen Corporation, Dell, Inc., PepsiCo Inc., Doubletree Hotels, and Pizza Hut.

Index

S

scrimmage, 112–113
self confidence, parental role in development of, 77, 78, 79
self-esteem, 77, 78
self-image, of children, 50
selfishness. *See* unselfishness
self-worth, 77, 78
skills
    assessment, by coach, 101–104
    heart, head, and hands framework of assessment, 104–105
success
    child's perspective, 56
    parental perspective, 56–57
summary of key points
    for coaches, 89, 96, 106, 116, 125
    for parents, 49, 58, 66, 73, 81
    for players, 9, 16, 23, 32, 40

T

talent
    assessment, by coach, 101–104
    heart, head, and hands framework of assessment, 104–105
team concept
    coach's role in developing, 94–95, 103–104
    usefulness of, 67
trustworthiness
    of coach, 100–101
    of players, 25–26

978-1-58348-764-8

1-58348-764-6

Printed in the United States
112818LV00004B/100-183/A